HOW TO INVEST ₹ 10,000 TO EARN ₹ 100 CRORES IN STOCK MARKET

HOW TO INVEST ₹ 10,000 TO EARN ₹ 100 CRORES IN STOCK MARKET

SHYAM SUNDAR GOEL

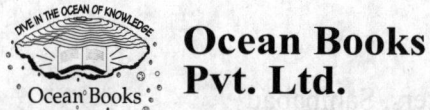

Ocean Books Pvt. Ltd.

No part of this publication can be reproduced, stored in a retrieval system or transmitted in any form or by any means, electronic, mechanical, photocopying, recording or otherwise, without the prior permission of the author and the publisher.

Published by
Ocean Books (P) Ltd.
4/19 Asaf Ali Road,
New Delhi-110 002 (INDIA)
e-mail: prabhatbooks@gmail.com

ISBN 978-81-8430-636-1
HOW TO INVEST ₹10,000 TO EARN ₹100 CRORES IN STOCK MARKET
by Shyam Sundar Goel

Edition
2024

Price
₹ 300.00 (Three Hundred only)

© Reserved

Printed at
Sanjay Printers, Sahibabad

To the investors, I hope this book will lead to become a billionaire.

Contents

1. Introduction 9
2. The Story of Summation 14
3. GDP of India 22
4. Basic Conditions of Stock Markets 27
5. What is a Stock Market? 34
6. Price To Earnings Ratio 40
7. Goal Setting 52
8. Why Should You Write Down Your Goals? ... 59
9. Smart Tips for Goal Setting 61
10. Mercedes Story 66
11. Benefits of Visualisation 84
12. Benefits of Stock Markets 88
13. Portable Profession 92
14. Market Capitalisation 139
15. Technical Analysis 144
16. Theory 1: Seasonal Products 172

17. Theory 2: Bill Gates 188
18. Theory 3: Premium Brands 195
19. Theory 4: Mass Consumption 198
20. Theory 5: Multi-bagger 202
21. Tips: How to Become a Billionaire? 206

1

Introduction

Dear reader, first of all I would like to thank you for buying this book. This is an amazing book written on stock markets. Thanks for choosing this book. Through this book, we will provide you five simple steps to turn your single investment of just ₹10,000 into ₹100 crores.

You have definitely spent some money to buy this book; however, I would like to assure you that the knowledge that you are going to gain out of this book would be much more valuable and the cost incurred by you would be quite insignificant compared to the same. We want to educate as many people as possible to enable them to invest in stock markets and become billionaires easily. Your decision to buy this book is the best decision of your life. There are very few good books on stock markets in India; however, they have explained the concepts in highly technical way and lot of complexities and difficulties are encountered in applying those concepts in the stock market. This book has been written with the aim of presenting the ideas to solve problems. Anybody may read and understand this book comfortably. After acquiring comprehensive knowledge on stock markets, I have conducted seminars to guide people, even students, on the subject. I have organised many public seminars for common people and school and college students.

I have developed a simple technique and formula for investment in stock markets. My students also appreciate that understanding the functioning of stock market is quite easy. I have devised some theories—basic theories that work quite effectively in the stock market. They work smoothly in India and, after conducting many workshops on them, I wish to present those theories in a book. My efforts are constrained by time. However, a book does not have any such limitation. It may be easily accessible to anybody. For me, it's a big challenge to conduct multiple seminars across India. This requires plenty of time and a lot of effort. I am not capable of training more than a lac of people in my entire lifetime. Our population is over 138 crores and more than 77 thousand births are taking place every day. There is great demand for education and hence, I have penned this book.

Introduction

Various surveys conducted across India reveal that more than 90% of investors in stock markets are incurring loss. I am writing this book to explain the art and science of making money in stock markets. There are around 1.60 crores Demat account holders in India; this is less than even 2% of the total population. Banks' interest rates are going down everyday and during the years in the last decade, the interest rates have been brought down from two digits to single digits. The interest rates that used to be around 12% some 15 years back are hovering between 6% and 7% now. The Indian economy is growing fast and we are going to be a part of G-8 nations. The interest rates in G-8 nations are just between 2% and 3%.

This declining income from interest year after year is creating problems for people. Suppose, a person earlier maintained a fixed deposit of ₹1 crore and was receiving interest of ₹12 lacs per year i.e. ₹1 lac per month. Now, in 2020, he gets only 6-7% pa interest. Inflation has already brought down the purchasing capacity of ₹1 lac to just ₹50,000, and his interest income is also reduced. We may hence say that he is actually getting ₹50000 towards interest and, taking into account the impact of inflation, his effective income is just ₹25000. Hence, a person who is holding his hard-earned money in his bank account has the only option of apportioning some percentage of his capital towards investment in stock markets to earn better returns.

We will provide you step-by-step guidance for making investments in stock markets. We are not suggesting you to transfer your entire capital to stock markets. We are just trying to convey that you should shift a part of your capital into stock markets and earn good returns.

More than 40% of people in developed countries invest in stock markets and earn great returns. The only way to make successful investments in stock markets is to acquire knowledge about the same. If you have good knowledge of the stock markets, there is no way you would incur loss there. We will try to explain in detail each and every aspect of the stock market. We are discussing here in brief. You may see the Sensex and NIFTY attaining new heights in the stock market. You may even watch the market and the stocks being controlled by bears and returns falling sharply; however, such falls in the market are temporary and they harm only the investors who lack good understanding of the market. Those who acquire proper knowledge of stock markets become capable of creating immense wealth and earning passive income from the markets.

While reading this book, you would need to underline important points and make small notes to memorise the ideas easily. That would help you to understand the entire book without opening it repeatedly.

To attain perfection in stock markets, you must impart this knowledge to at least two other persons. This will help you to become perfect in stock market investments. You would also be adding values to others' lives by doing this.

Introduction

I also assure you that the value you reap out of this book would be more than the price that you have paid for buying the book. The path is open for you to become a multimillionaire and a billionaire; our best wishes are with you!

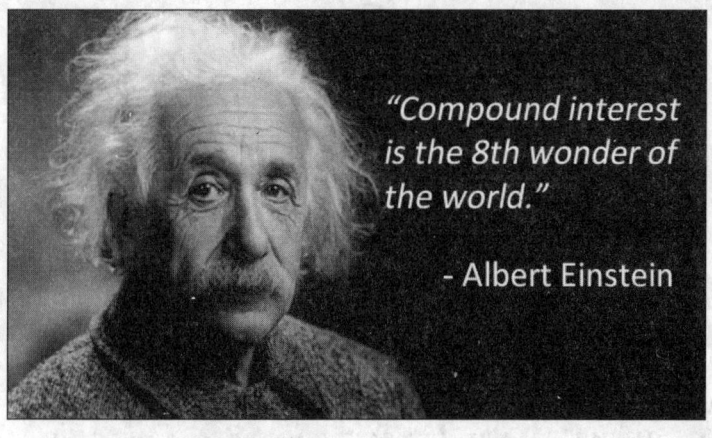

2

The Story of Summation

There was a king who once organised a chess tournament. A winner was declared and he asked the winner what the latter desired to have as his award. The winner very humbly said, 'Just a few grains of rice." He further explained that he wanted a grain of rice to be placed in the first square of the chess, two grains in the next, four grains in the third and so on up to the 64th square, and he just wanted to have the number of grains that is computed for the 64th square.

The king replied, "I am quite pleased with you. Why are you asking only for some grains of rice? You may

The Story of Summation

seek anything as your award." However, the winner held on to his decision. The king asked for the counting of grains. The number that was arrived at for the 64th square was -

92,23,37,20,36,85,47,80,000

This 19-digit figure was in crores. We have seven digits in a crore. It's just difficult to read this number. We have however decoded this number as -

92 sankh 23 padma 37 nil 20 kharab 36 arab 85 crore 47 lakh 80 thousand.

The king had to lose his kingdom, as he did not realise the power of summation. There are many examples where people have accumulated wealth using stock markets. For example, the wealth that Warren Buffet has created through stock markets is around 57,54,00,00,00,000/- that comes to almost 6 lakh crores.

Shri Rakesh Jhunjhunwala has made ₹20,000 crores from stock markets.

Shri Radhakrishna Damani has earned more than ₹90,000 crores from stock markets and he is now the second richest person in India.

Shri Raamdeo Agrawal has created wealth of ₹3000 crores using stock markets.

Shri Vijay Kedia has made more that ₹1000 crores in stock markets.

Smt Dolly Khanna has created wealth of ₹1000 crores through stock markets. She had started investing at the age of 52.

Shri Warren Buffet had started investing at the age of just 11 years. Age is no bar for making money or earning profits in stock markets.

These are just a few examples where people earned several crores of rupees from stock markets. A person owning properties worth ₹100 crores is known as a billionaire. We are going to explain plenty of methods and techniques to become a billionaire using stock markets. We wish to educate the maximum number of people in our country and help them understand the techniques of investing in stock markets and easily become billionaires. We want to make some billionaires in our country in order to make our country the greatest power in the world. I have a dream that one day India will become 100% literate. As our economy grows, education would become easily accessible to poor children.

Before we delve into real stock markets, we will talk about Warren Buffet, who is a shining example for many people to start investing and making money in stock markets. We will then discuss some facts about our economy to understand how it works. After that, we will explore workings of stock markets and then discuss the four techniques of investments in stock markets that may help anybody to easily become a billionaire.

The Story of Summation

These are the most important aspects before entering a stock market. When we take up farming, we first of all clean the field and then start cultivation. We need to understand some basic principles before we start investing in the market. This is quite important. You should invest in stock markets only after you understand all these basic things.

You run the risk of withdrawal if you enter the market without understanding the basic principles. Many people are making mistakes and incurring huge losses in the market. If you wish to generate wealth in the stock market and create regular passive income out of the same, you need to go through this book very carefully and underline the points that are most relevant for you. You would also have to create short notes for your relevant goals. You may not need to go through the entire book again in future.

I am making this appeal again. If you go through this book, you would be able to easily understand the art and science of investing in stock markets. Please don't skip any page of any chapter in the book. It's very important to understand the market. You need to follow three rules while reading this book:

Rule 1: Read the entire book,

Rule 2: Underline the points that you would like to refer to repeatedly,

Rule 3: Make a short note to avoid going through the

entire book again when you need to refer to any specific point, thus saving you time.

You must educate at least two other persons with the help of this book. There are benefits of sharing knowledge. When you teach others to improve their knowledge of stock markets, they raise many questions during the process. This automatically keeps the book getting revised. There is one more benefit. Those people would raise queries about the market. When you respond to them, it would actually help you understand the subject better. Another benefit arising out of the process is that you would be adding values to the lives of others. When you give something to others, it opens a door for you to receive something from the Universe. We should always strive to contribute to others' lives. The stock market is a real concept to assist in making money and improving economy in the world. You would be able to understand the things better once you finish reading this book.

Shri Warren Buffet has created wealth of US $ 8220 crores (till March 2019) using stock markets.

We are great followers of Warren Buffet. By generating immense wealth from the stock markets, he has taught a lesson to the world that anybody may not only make money in the market but also make the money work for him.

US $ 8220 crores i.e. ₹5,75,400 crores (assuming 1 Dollar to be equal to 70 rupees) in 75 years! His current age is 90 years and he started investing at the age of just 11 years. This means that, after learning a lot, he took 75 years to accumulate that wealth of ₹6 lakh crores. He had to learn everything on his own, but the secret of making money in the stock market is now out in the open.

It would not take 75 years now for anybody to make that much money. He would need much less time for the same. There are many new examples and strategies that, if applied, would help anybody to create huge wealth in a short time.

In this book, we will share many examples for making money. As you are aware, we have assigned the title 'How to use stock markets to become billionaire?' to this book. This is not a joke. We will share that secret how anybody would be able to generate crores of rupees by investing just ₹10,000 in the market. In India, you may learn a lot from Rakesh Jhunjhunwala who started with an investment of ₹5,000 only and was able to earn ₹15,000 crores from equity stock markets.

This book would help you understand the fundamental principles of the stock market easily. Not only the basic concepts, you may even understand technical points comfortably. We will share with you how you may be able to easily turn your investment of just ₹10,000 into ₹100 crores. This is an amazing book that provides a lot of information about equity markets.

It's our dream to make our country prosperous. We want to use equity markets to create a number of billionaires, each with riches beyond ₹100 crores. We dream of a 100% literate country. If our country creates crores of billionaires, who on their own come forward to donate a part of their fortune for education of poor children, we would achieve 100% literacy in our country one day. With these words, let's start reading the book. We wish that your dream of becoming a billionaire came true.

Fundamentals of Economy

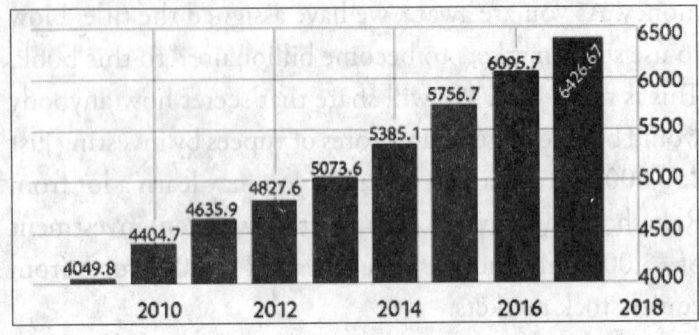

Purchasing Power Per Person in India

- ❖ 1,120 in 1990
- ❖ 1,960 in 2000
- ❖ 7,060 in 2017

India's Purchasing Power Parity

Definition

This figure provides value of Gross Domestic Product or all the final goods and services produced in a country during a year. The GDP of a country in terms of PPP exchange rate is the value of all the goods and services produced in the country evaluated for the current year at prevailing rates of United Nations. Most of the economists prefer to treat this as a way to measure the extent of welfare per head and to compare the living conditions or utilisation of resources at different locations in the country. It's difficult to measure this, as all the goods and services in the country are valued in US Dollars even when no distinct price for such goods and services may be available in USA (e.g. price of a bullock-cart or a non-American defence equipment). As a result, for some countries, PPPs are computed based on small and sometimes even different sets of goods and services. Besides this, many countries officially keep away from the PPP projects of the World Bank that make such computations. Hence, there may be some margin of error in the estimation of GDP for those countries. For many developing countries, the measure of PPP based GDP is a factor for determination of their official exchange rates. For most of the rich industrial countries, there is generally not much of difference in their GDP measures.

❏❏

3

GDP of India

❖ In 1990 - USD 32,660.80 crores (22,86,200 crores)
❖ In 2000 - USD 47,469.16 crores (33,36,830 crores)
❖ In 2018 - USD 2,689.99 arabs (1,88,23,000 arabs)

What is GDP?

Gross Domestic Products (GDP) means the sum total of all the final goods and services produced in a country, expressed 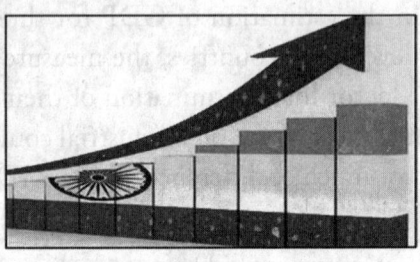 in terms of money, during a specific period, generally an year. This is an important macro economic parameter in the form of an indicator of the capacity as well as efficiency of the economy.

This is so because GDP is significantly linked to most of the other socio-economic indicators like poverty, unemployment, standard of living and even literacy and standard of health. In most of the cases, the correlation is in marginal or incremental basis.

Consistently growing GDP has the potential of making a positive impact on the poverty, health services, literacy, employment etc. in the economy. Hence, the concept of GDP is important to understand the economic well being of a state.

How to Calculate GDP?

The following formula is used to calculate GDP:

GDP = Private expenditures + gross investments + government investments + government spending + (imports - exports).

GDP deflator is quite important, as the same measures price inflation.

This is calculated by dividing Nominal GDP by Real GDP and then multiplying by 100 (based on the formula).

Demat system was launched in 1996 through the 'Act of Depository'.

In 2008: approximately 2.91 million Demat account holders.

In 2018: approximately 16.70 million Demat account holders.

What is a Dematerialisation Account?

Investing in equity stocks in physical form involves a lengthy process, lot of paper work and risk of receiving fake stocks. A Demat account is needed to keep the entire experience easy and streamlined. When trading online, A Demat account is used for holding stocks and securities in dematerialised/electronic form. Under dematerialisation, your share certificates are converted from physical form to electronic form to facilitate their accessibility.

What are the Facilities Provided by Demat Account?

Easy Transfer of Shares

A Demat account may be used for transfer of share holding of an investor. This is done by using a 'Delivery Instruction Slip' (DIS) in order to conduct share trading. You may provide all relevant information in this slip for smooth execution of the transaction.

Loan Against Securities

Securities held in your Demat account can give you access to different kinds of loans provided by banks. You may pledge such holdings as collateral security for availing loans from banks.

Dematerialisation and Dematerialisation

If you hold a Demat account, converting your securities in different forms becomes easy. You may issue necessary instructions to your Depository Participant (DP) for dematerialisation i.e. conversion of physical share certificates into electronic forms. Conversely, you may even get your electronic securities converted into physical forms as per your requirements.

Easy and Multiple Access Options

Being an electronic facility, multiple mediums may be used to access your Demat account. You may use your computer, smartphone or other handheld devices with Internet facility to carry out your investment, trade, monitoring and other security related transactions.

Receiving Share Dividends and Other Profits Related to Corporate Actions

Demat account facilitates the process of receiving benefits arising out of ownership of your securities. Whenever a company issues dividends, interest or refunds to its investors, all Demat account holders automatically receive such benefits. Besides this, corporate actions like stock splits, rights issue or bonus issue are automatically updated in Demat accounts of the shareholders.

Liquidity of Shares

Demat account has made the process of receiving proceeds of sale of stocks quite easy, fast and comfortable.

Blocked Demat Account

Demat account holders may freeze specific type or quantity of securities in his account. He may even choose the option of freezing his Demat account for any specific period. This will stop transfer of amount from any debit or credit card into that Demat account.

Globalisation of India

Demat accounts have played a significant role in providing foreign investors access to Indian stock markets and rise in foreign investments in stock markets has helped in improving the overall Indian economy.

❑❑

4

Basic Conditions of Stock Markets

Bombay Stock Exchange (BSE)

The Bombay Stock Exchange (BSE) is the first and the largest securities market of India and was established in the year 1957 as the Native Shares and Stock Brokers' Association. Based in Mumbai, India, BSE lists close to 6000 companies and is one the largest exchanges in the world, along with New York Stock Exchange (NYSE), NASDAQ, London Stock Exchange Group, Japan Exchange Group and Shanghai Stock Exchange.

The BSE has helped in developing retail debt market as well as capital markets in the country and has also been instrumental in development of the Indian corporate sector.

How does BSE Work?

In 1995, BSE switched from an open-floor to an electronic trading system. There are more than a dozen of electronic exchanges in USA alone. The New York Stock Exchange and NASDAQ are most widely known. Today, electronic systems dominate the financial industry. This provides better efficiency with minimal errors and fast execution as compared to traditional open-outcry trading systems.

The securities listed on BSE include stocks, stock futures, stock options, index futures, index options and weekly options. Overall performance of BSE is measured by SENSEX, a benchmark index based on 30 out the BSE's largest stocks covering 12 sectors.

30 Companies in BSE SENSEX as on 30 June 2019

Company	CMP	Market Cap
Yes Bank Ltd.(L)	88.2	22,319
Tata Motors Ltd.(L)	160.2	47,699
Hero Moto Corp Ltd.(L)	2,514	52,046
Tata Steel Ltd.(L)	478.1	59,646
Vedanta Ltd.(L)	163.6	63,601
Tech Mahindra Ltd.(L)	681.5	67,611
Mahindra & Mahindra Ltd.(L)	642.3	83,531

Basic Conditions of Stock Markets

Bajaj Auto Ltd.(L)	2,838	83,788
IndusInd Bank Ltd.(L)	1,532	90,094
Sun Pharmaceutical Industries Ltd.(L)	375.1	94,078
Power Grid Corporation of India Ltd.(L)	205.8	1,09,942
Asian Paints Ltd.(L)	1,358	1,30,432
HCL Technologies Ltd.(L)	1,017	1,41,114
NTPC Ltd.(L)	136.4	1,41,838
Bharti Airtel Ltd.(L)	364.9	1,86,050
Maruti Suzuki India Ltd.(L)	6,365	1,97,621
Oil & Natural Gas Corporation Ltd.(L)	161.2	2,10,216
Axis Bank Ltd.(L)	806	2,11,834
Bajaj Finance Ltd.(L)	3,719	2,16,364
Larsen & Toubro Ltd.(L)	1,557	2,20,538
ICICI Bank Ltd.(L)	436.2	2,81,317
Kotak Mahindra Bank Ltd.(L)	1,518	2,85,980
Infosys Ltd.(L)	718.2	3,14,801
State Bank Of India(L)	370.6	3,27,800
ITC Ltd.(L)	279.4	3,40,671
Hindustan Unilever Ltd.(L)	1,791	3,87,976
Housing Development Finance Corporation Ltd.(L)	2,279	3,93,542
HDFC Bank Ltd.(L)	2,475	6,78,735
Reliance Industries Ltd.(L)	1,263	8,13,304
Tata Consultancy Services Ltd.(L)	2,162	8,41,510

National Stock Exchange (NSE)

The National Stock Exchange of India Ltd (NSE) is the leading stock exchange of India located in Mumbai. The NSE was established in 1992 as the first dematerialised stock exchange in the country. The NSE was the first exchange of the country to provide a modern, fully automated screen-based electronic trading system that offered easy trading facilities to the investors spread across the length and breadth of the country.

The National Stock Exchange has a total market capitalization of more than US$2.27 trillion, making it the world's 11th-largest stock exchange as of April 2018. NSE's flagship index, the NIFTY 50, a 50 stock index is used extensively by investors in India and around the world as a barometer of the Indian capital market. The NIFTY 50 index was launched by NSE in 1996. However, Vaidyanathan (2016) estimates that only about 4% of the Indian economy / GDP is actually derived from the stock exchanges in India.

Unlike countries like the United States where nearly 70% of the country's GDP is derived from large companies in the corporate sector, the corporate sector in India accounts for only 12-14% of the national GDP (as of October 2016). Of these only 7,800 companies are listed of which only 4000 trade on the stock exchanges at BSE and NSE. Hence the stocks traded at the BSE and NSE account for only around 4% of the Indian economy, which derives most of its income-related activity from the so-called unorganized sector and household spending.

NIFTY 50 is a diversified 50 stock index representing 13 sectors of the economy. It is used for different purposes like benchmarking funds portfolio, index-based derivatives and index funds. NIFTY 50 is owned and managed by NSE Indices Ltd (previously known as India Index Services & Products Limited). NSE Indices is a specialised Indian company that is focussed on indices as its main products.

As on 29 March 2019, NIFTY 50 represented approximately 66.8% of free float market capitalisation of the stocks listed on NSE.

Total value of trades in NIFTY 50 constituents during six months ending with March 2019 was approximately 53.40% of the value of trades in all the stocks listed on NSE.

NIFTY 50 Stocks as on 30 June 2019

	Company Name	CMP	Market Cap (Cr.)
1.	Indiabulls Housing Finance Ltd. (L)	727	30,099
2.	Yes Bank Ltd.(L)	88.2	22,319
3.	Zee Entertainment Enterprises Ltd.(L)	345.8	34,232

4.	Dr. Reddys Laboratories Ltd.(L)	2,601	43,239
5.	Cipla Ltd.(L)	550	44,437
6.	Hindalco Industries Ltd.(L)	198.9	46,433
7.	Tata Motors Ltd.(L)	160.2	47,699
8.	Bharti Infratel Ltd.(L)	260.9	48,682
9.	Hero MotoCorp Ltd.(L)	2,514	52,046
10.	UPL Ltd.(L)	666.3	53,336
11.	Eicher Motors Ltd.(L)	19,627	54,064
12.	Tata Steel Ltd.(L)	478.1	59,646
13.	Grasim Industries Ltd.(L)	925	61,937
14.	Vedanta Ltd.(L)	163.6	63,601
15.	JSW Steel Ltd.(L)	266.6	66,486
16.	Tech Mahindra Ltd.(L)	681.5	67,611
17.	Britannia Industries Ltd.(L)	2,824	68,289
18.	GAIL (India) Ltd.(L)	306.5	69,389
19.	Bharat Petroleum Corporation Ltd.(L)	369.6	82,399
20.	Mahindra & Mahindra Ltd.(L)	642.3	83,531
21.	Bajaj Auto Ltd.(L)	2,838	83,788
22.	Adani Ports and Special Economic Zone Ltd.(L)	402.6	85,996
23.	IndusInd Bank Ltd.(L)	1,532	90,094
24.	Sun Pharmaceutical Industries Ltd.(L)	375.1	94,078
25.	Power Grid Corporation Of India Ltd.(L)	205.8	1,09,942
26.	Titan Company Ltd.(L)	1,278	1,14,582
27.	Ultratech Cement Ltd.(L)	4,521	1,27,563

28.	Asian Paints Ltd.(L)	1,358	1,30,432
29.	Bajaj Finserv Ltd.(L)	8,438	1,36,009
30.	HCL Technologies Ltd.(L)	1,017	1,41,114
31.	NTPC Ltd.(L)	136.4	1,41,838
32.	Indian Oil Corporation Ltd.(L)	152.2	1,47,426
33.	Coal India Ltd.(L)	241.9	1,54,808
34.	Wipro Ltd.(L)	271.9	1,71,284
35.	Bharti Airtel Ltd.(L)	364.9	1,86,050
36.	Maruti Suzuki India Ltd.(L)	6,365	1,97,621
37.	Oil & Natural Gas Corporation Ltd.(L)	161.2	2,10,216
38.	Axis Bank Ltd.(L)	806	2,11,834
39.	Bajaj Finance Ltd.(L)	3,719	2,16,364
40.	Larsen & Toubro Ltd.(L)	1,557	2,20,538
41.	ICICI Bank Ltd.(L)	436.2	2,81,317
42.	Kotak Mahindra Bank Ltd.(L)	1,518	2,85,980
43.	Infosys Ltd.(L)	718.2	3,14,801
44.	State Bank Of India(L)	370.6	3,27,800
45.	ITC Ltd.(L)	279.4	3,40,671
46.	Hindustan Unilever Ltd.(L)	1,791	3,87,976
47.	Housing Development Finance Corporation Ltd.(L)	2,279	3,93,542
48.	HDFC Bank Ltd.(L)	2,475	6,78,735
49.	Reliance Industries Ltd.(L)	1,263	8,13,304
50.	Tata Consultancy Services Ltd.(L)	2,162	8,41,510
			1,453,431

❏❏

5

What is a Stock Market?

I will take you to the world of stock markets in this article. First of all, let's understand what a stock market is. A stock market is the place where shares are traded. A share of any company represents a unit of ownership of that company. For instance, if you buy 10 shares of ABC Company at the rate of ₹200 per share, you become a shareholder of the company. You may sell those shares of ABC anytime. Investing in stocks may help you realise your dreams like higher education, buying a car, building a house etc. If you start investing at an early age and stay invested for a long period, you may achieve high returns. You may develop your investment strategy based on the time you need money.

What is a Stock Market?

By buying shares, you are actually investing money in the company. As the company grows, value of your shares too will goes up. You may make profit by selling those shares in the market. There are many factors that impact the price of a share. The price may sometimes rise while it may fall some other times. Long term investment will nullify the fall in price.

Why at all does a company sells its shares to the public? A company requires capital or funds for its expansion, development etc. and hence it raises funds from public. The process that the company uses for issue of shares is known as 'Initial Public Offer' (IPO). We will learn more about IPO under Primary Market.

You might have heard people talking about the bull market and bear market. What do they mean? A bull market is the one where the prices of stocks keep rising and a bear market is where the prices keep falling. Where are they traded? At the NSE (National Stock Exchange) and the BSE (Bombay Stock Exchange). They are the two major stock exchanges in India and are regulated by SEBI (Securities and Exchange Board of India). Brokers act as an intermediary between stock exchanges and investors and hence, you would need to open a Demat account and Trading account with a broker before starting investing or trading in stocks. You may easily open a Demat account online using a simple process. You may start your investment journey after linking your bank account with the above accounts.

Two Kinds of Stock Markets

Stock markets have been classified into two namely:
1. Offline Market
2. Secondary Market

Primary Market

A company or government raises money by issuing shares in the primary market through the process of IPO.

- ❖ The issue may be made through public or private placement.
- ❖ An issue is treated as public issue when shares are issued to more than 200 individuals. It is treated as a private issue if shares are allotted to less than 200 individuals.
- ❖ The price of a share may be based on Fixed Price or Book building issue; the issuer determines the Fixed Price and mentions the same in its offer document. Book building is where the price of an issue is determined based on the demand from the investors.

Secondary Market

The stocks bought in the primary market may be sold in the secondary market. The secondary market is operated through Over the Counter (OTC) and Exchange Traded markets. OTC markets are informal markets where two parties agree on trades to be settled in future.

Exchange traded markets are highly regulated. It is also sometimes called auction market where all transactions happen via the exchange.

What is a Share?

Definition & meaning: A share is a single unit of ownership in a company or financial asset. It is essentially an exchangeable piece of value of a company, which can fluctuate up or down, depending on several different market factors. Companies divide capital into shares as a means of raising capital. Shares are also known as stocks. There are two main types of shares: one, common shares, which people call ordinary shares, and the other, preference shares.

There are two main types of shares.

1. **Ordinary share (Common Stock):** This entitles the shareholder to share in the profits of the company and to right of vote in annual general meetings and other official meetings of the company.
2. **Preference Share (Favourite Stocks):** This entitles the shareholder to a definite periodic income (interest) but generally does not provide any voting rights.

Definition of Market Capitalisation

Definition

Market capitalisation of a company is the total value of the company's outstanding shares at current market price.

It's calculated by multiplying the current market price of the company's share with the number of total outstanding shares.

Details

Market capitalisation is one of the most significant features that helps investors in determining the risk and return for a share. This also helps investors to identify the stocks that satisfy their risk and diversification criteria. For instance, suppose a company has 2 crore outstanding shares and the current market price per share is ₹100. The company's market capitalisation is hence 2,00,00,000 × 100 = ₹200 crores. There are three kinds of shares of companies.

Large Cap: Stocks of the companies having market cap equal to or over ₹10,000 crores.

Mid Cap: Stocks of companies having market cap between ₹2 crores and ₹10 crores.

Small Cap: Stocks of companies having market cap below ₹2 crores.

Definition of Earning Per Share (EPS)

Earning Per Share (EPS) is an important financial measure that reflects the profitability of a company. This is calculated by dividing the net profit of the company by the number of all outstanding shares. This is an instrument that is often used by market participants to assess the profitability of a company before buying its shares.

What is a Stock Market?

1. **Weighted Average Per Share (Net Profit after Tax-Details):** EPS is the share of profit of the company that is allotted to each individual unit of its stocks. This is a term that is quite significant for investors and traders. The more the EPS of a company in the stock market, the more would be its profit. It is appropriate to use the weighted average while calculating EPS, as the number of outstanding shares keeps changing with time. EPS may be computed in two ways.

2. **Earning Per Share:** (Net earnings after tax - Preferred Dividend) / The weighted average number of outstanding shares. In a finer form, convertible shares as well as warrants are also included with outstanding shares. This is considered to be a more expanded edition of the basic return per share. For an investor, who is primarily interested in a stable source of income, EPS may provide information about the direction that the company has adopted for improving its dividends. However, EPS is an important instrument for the investors and it should not be looked at otherwise. For a more informed and prudent decision, the EPS of a company should always be seen in comparison with other companies.

❏❏

6

Price To Earnings Ratio

Price to earnings ratio (PE Ratio) is a measure of the current share price relative to its annual per share net earnings. PE Ratio represents the current level of investors' demand for the company share. High PE Ratio generally indicates high demand as investors expect growth in company's income in future. PE ratio has units of years, which can be interpreted as the number of years of earnings to pay back purchase price.

PR ratio is often referred to as the 'multiple' because it demonstrates how much an investor is willing to pay for one rupee of earnings. PE Ratios are sometimes calculated using estimations of next year's earnings per share in the denominator. When this happens, it is usually noted.

Price To Earnings Ratio

Formula: Price to Earnings Ratio = Price / Earnings Per Share (EPS)

$$\text{PE Ratio} = \frac{\text{Earning per share}}{\text{Price per share}}$$

Calculation of Book Value for Estimation of Value of Your Business

To run your business, you likely rely on assets such as equipment, your building, your company car, inventory and cash, and if you wish to maintain your books, you should create financial statements and determine theoretical value of your property. You need to calculate book value.

What is Book Value?

Book value, also called value or net book value, is an asset's original cost minus its depreciation. An asset's original cost goes beyond the ticket price of the item - original cost includes as asset's purchase price and the cost of setting it up (e.g. transportation and installation). Depreciation is the decrease of an asset's value on account of general wear and tear.

You may also arrive at the book value of a company by subtracting intangible assets (non-physical items of value) and liabilities from total assets. Calculating the book value of your small business indicates how much your company would be worth if you were to liquidate your assets. An asset's book value is its theoretical value, not the amount it would fetch in the current market. If you want to know how much an asset would sell for, you need to calculate its fair market value. The book value may be higher, lower or equal to an asset's fair market value.

Generally, you can't find the absolute book value of your intangible assets like intellectual property and reputation of your business. You should use book value to find the worth of your tangible assets.

Purpose of Calculating Book Value

Why should you calculate the book value of your assets or small business?

If you are seeking outside financing, you may need to calculate the book value of your assets and business. Investors and lenders need to invest or lend money before knowing the worth of your property.

Shareholders may also want to know how much they would receive if you were to liquidate an asset or all your assets. If you structure your business as a corporate, you may have to find the book value for your shareholders.

You may also find the book value of an asset that you want to sell. You need to know the original cost and consider the book value of an asset to determine its fair market value.

Another reason you may wish to find an asset's book value is to compare it to its fair market value. By comparing book value against market value, you may determine if the asset is under or over priced in the market.

How to Calculate Book Value?

How do you calculate book value?

The formula you use depends on whether you are trying to find an asset's carrying value or book value of your small business.

Example:

First of all, we need to find out the equity of shareholders, which is the difference between total assets and liabilities (loans and other liabilities), i.e.

36,16,433,00 − (39, 91,257.62 + 3,19,701.42) = 2,09,473.96.

Price determination and even when you wish to personally invest in real estate, you would get appreciation in the value of your property and you would additionally get rental income that would be yearly based.

What is Appreciation?

Appreciation, in general terms, is an increase in the value of a share over time. The increase may occur for a number of reasons, including increased demand or weakening supply. In such a situation, the price of the share would increase or appreciate.

In the stock market, the price of your share would increase or appreciate and you would also receive dividends from time to time.

What is Dividend?

A dividend is a share of profits and a company retains the earnings paid out to its shareholders. When a company generates profit and accumulates retained earnings, those earnings may be either reinvested in the business or paid out to shareholders as dividend. The annual dividend per share divided by the share price is the dividend yield.

How does a Dividend Work?

A dividend's value is determined on per-share basis and is paid equally to all shareholders of the same class (common, preferred etc.). The payment has to be approved by the Board of Directors. When a dividend is declared, it will then be paid on a specific date known as the payable date.

How does it Work?

1. The company generates profits and retains earnings.
2. The management team decides some excess profits should be paid out to its shareholders (instead of reinvesting in business).
3. The board approves the proposed dividend.

4. The company announces the dividend (the amount per share, the date when it is to be paid, record date etc.)
5. The dividend is paid to the shareholders.

How does Your Model Help You Make a Sell Decision?

Generally, we sell an item that we call a product. This could come up in many ways. We look at the stocks that have done very well and normally enter into these when they are not well covered by different research analysts or gain much coverage in the media. They are in a sense out of favour even though they are making 52-week highs. But many times, when we are into these positions after a few years, we find that there is a sense of over-ownership. A lot of people have got into these stocks. The CEO is coming on magazine covers.

There is an interview a day. They are on CNBC or other channels regularly. We call that magazine cover syndrome. When there is whole bunch of euphoria, we start lighting up our positions, as we think a lot is built into the price at that point. Similarly, if you look at a lot of research coverage from the sell side, we tend to think that a lot of - if the numbers are so well-known, its in the price. Based on your model, give us your assessment of where the market is placed right now. We are so process-driven that we don't have to be pre-emptive about the market. It is ultimately a bottom-up stock picker game. It's about finding great businesses at right prices. That's the essence of it and that doesn't change. This method helps you get that multi-bagger.

The aim of doing this is to find those winners - those 7x, 8x, 10x in three, four or five years or more time than that. So, the market direction is one element of it. I would say that's something we focus the least on, to be very honest.

How do You Play Demographics as an Investor?

In India, the power of demographics is so large, it can have a big impact on almost everything. If you look at the fundamental principles of this bull market, what are they based on - food, clothing, shelter, financial services, very simple things. In this respect, we are a very simple market. There is nothing so complex about it. There is a basic want and need for goods and services. As per capita moves upwards, as we double over the next decade, there will be change in demographics. People will want more and more.

Everybody wants more and more and better - better quality of services, a better home, better food, more nutrition, simple things. We in fact believe in keeping things simple. As an investor, there are going to be so many opportunities. These days, there is an opportunity every month. Look at D-Mart. It did not exist in the capital market and now...what does it provide? A simple service at a very competitive cost in the most efficient manner is possible; a very scalable, well executed business model and all of a sudden, you have market cap of around ₹60,000 crores created from something quite simple. There could be many more stories like this. We just need to be open to them. Businesses have a moat, but these moats can be breached easily because of technology. Do you agree?

Of course, technology can breach moats. There is no doubt about that; but as far as technology and India are concerned, we are an adaptor. We are a user at this point. The entrepreneurs and the companies seem to be very technology adaptor-oriented, very process-driven, making efficiency simple - providing simple processes and improving processes and delivering to the consumer in a very simple and improved way. I don't think we are there in terms of being disruptive. The Indian market is very simple at this point.

Combination of Growth and Non-cyclicality

One key factor that creates value in the stock market is consistent growth in economic and market cycles. While market values growth, it places even greater premium on consistency in growth. Most of multi-baggers are generally high growth companies in non-cyclical businesses. It's extremely rare to find a multi-bagger in a typical commodity business like steel, aluminium or even oil. Economic cycles dissipate most of the wealth of these companies. It is also hard for a staid utility company to become a multi-bagger, as it operates in a very constricted atmosphere.

Efficient Utilisation of Capital

There are different ways to approach shareholder returns; while there are several measures of capital utilisation, two of the key measures are Return on Capital Employed (ROCE) and Return on Equity (ROE). ROCE measures the overall returns for all stakeholders and is a relatively good measure of the overall efficiency of the company. A consistently low ROCE signifies that there is something wrong with the business or the company. ROE is a measure of shareholders return and a very important parameter for the investors. Some of the best wealth creators have very high ROE and ROCE relative to the rest of the industry. Typically, companies with high ROCE and ROE would also be generating positive free cash flows consistently, for which markets are willing to pay a premium.

When we look back at the markets over the past few decades, scores of multi-baggers have come in the Indian markets. Even if we consider a much shorter time frame post the global financial crisis in 2009, there have been numerous instances wherein small & mid cap stocks have multiplied wealth many times over on their way to become large cap stocks. That brings us to the core question of how to pick multi bagger stocks? Let's look at a very interesting 5-point model here.

Low Debt and an Asset-light Business Model is the Key to Wealth

It becomes difficult to find multi baggers from sectors like metals, infrastructure and utilities. One of the reasons for the same is the capital-intensive business model which leads to very high profit and low return ratios. High leverage increases insolvency risk in economic down cycles; but when debt is low, the entire issue of financial risk is overcome. It is not necessary to be a zero-debt company as some amount of leverage may actually improve shareholders returns. On the other hand, very high leverage may actually end up destroying shareholders value.

High Standards of Corporate Governance

Markets place great emphasis on corporate governance and are willing to pay a premium for the same. Some of the key traits of companies with good corporate governance are:

❖ Alignment of management interest with minority shareholders

❖ Very high standards of disclosure of shareholder related information. In fact, Narayana Murthy best summed up this sentiment with his famous words, "When in doubt, just disclose".

A good company may not always be a great stock to buy.

A great company with an impeccable pedigree may not always be a good stock to buy. This could be due to the fact that most of the triggers are already in the price and future growth potential does not justify the valuations. The PEG ratio (which is PE ratio divided by sustainable growth) is a simple way to measure valuation relative to growth. However, one needs to consider other parameters like return ratios and brands that the company has created which can go a long way in determining potential valuation. While there is no guarantee that the above-mentioned parameters would always help investors identify multi baggers, but they will surely go a long way in helping investors to avoid companies that may end up being value destructors.

	Company Name	Stock Price 10 Years Back	Current Stock Price	10 Years Change in Price	CAGR Return	P/E Ratio 10 Years Back	P/E Ratio Now
1.	Eicher Motors Ltd.	250	16,232	6,383%	52 %	3	53
2.	Lupin Ltd.	77	1,812	2,267%	37%	33	39
3.	Aurobindo Pharma Ltd.	40	825	1,981%	35%	19	29
4.	IndusInd Bank Ltd.	57	940	1,558	32%	9	28
5.	Asian Paints Ltd.	54	844	1,462%	32%	30	52

Price To Earnings Ratio

6.	Divis Laboratories Ltd.	75	1,137	1,425%	31%	29	35
7.	Kotak Mahindra Bank Ltd.	54	687	1,162%	29%	39	41
8.	LIC Housing Finance Ltd.	41	484	1,091%	28%	12	18
9.	Titan Company Ltd.	34	378	1,011%	27%	138	41
10.	Sun Pharmaceutical Ind. Ltd.	69	730	964%	27%	32	45
11.	Godrej Consumer Products Ltd.	120	1,251	946%	26%	25	42
12.	Dabur India Ltd.	29	279	865%	25%	32	42

7

Goal Setting

Goal Setting for Stock Market

There are many books as well as many research papers available on goals.  We will have to provide you some guidance on goals, as this is an important aspect of life. We will discuss on some important points relating to goals to enable you to easily understand your goals while entering the market.

Benefits of Goals

Goal destinations are the things that are important for you. There is one more word for the same - ambitions. However, ambition sounds like something that is beyond your understanding, whereas goal destinations are realistically achievable. If you are trying to work for them, what exactly you want to do with your life? Which are those important things that you would like to accomplish with your life? What is it that you would really regret not doing if you suddenly come to know that you had a limited amount of time left on the earth? Each of these things is a goal. Define each goal destination in one sentence. If any of the goals is a stepping stone for another goal, remove the same from the list, as it's not a goal destination.

Focus on what's Important

❖ Clear focus.

❖ Properly thought of and stated. Goals clearly determine your intentions and desires; the things that you really want to achieve.

Optimum Use of Resources

There are never enough resources to do everything, hence setting goals may help you to prioritise. Place your resources behind what you really want to do, rather than on things you are doing by default or by deflection.

Effective Use of Time

No doubt time is a resource, but it deserves special consideration, as it is so important. As Peter Drucker says,

"If you want to improve how you manage time - stop doing what doesn't need to be done."

Peace of Mind

Too often you can have many things in your mind. Writing down your goals can help you take all those ideas, apply perspective and priority and then motivate you into commitment and action.

Clarity in Decision Making

Knowing what you are trying to do means you can now ask, "Does this activity take me closer to my goal?"

Easy Measurement of What You Do

Setting goals, especially smart and soft goals, allows you to measure how effectively you are moving towards achieving them.

Easy Communication with Others

Setting goals enables you to clarify with others what you are trying to do, and hence what they need to do to contribute or support.

- ❖ Take some time now to think about what benefits you would gain from goal setting. How would they motivate you to achieve them?

Provides Control Over Your Future

The first change that we have to bring about for a better future is perception. Why perception? Because, our perception is our reality.

For example, if I consider my relationship as broken ignoring the feelings of my friend, it is my reality. My thoughts and feelings would induce me to do things as if the relationship is broken. Assuming that my relationship is not broken, I would need to change my perception about my relationship in order to change my thoughts and actions relating to the same.

When I change my perception, I see how I think and feel and my feelings and actions are in my control. When I believe that I have control over myself and I go for a healthy change, my worries get lightened, as I am in control of my life and not out of control.

I start looking at the world with the same basic amazement under this new perspective of life just as I used to see the world. I see a world with beauty. The biggest change is that now, I am looking at the positive aspects of the world more than from a single viewpoint. This provides me motivation.

Meaning

Motivation is an important factor that encourages people to give their best performance and helps them to reach their business goals. A strong positive motivation will enable increased output of employees; however, a negative motivation would weaken their performance. A key element in personnel management is motivation.

According to Likert, "It's the core of management that shows that every human being gives him a sense of worth in face-to-face groups which are most important to him. A supervisor should strive to treat individuals with dignity and a recognition for their personal worth."

1. Motivation is an inner feeling that energises a person to work more. The emotions or desires of a person prompt him to do a particular work. There are unsatisfied needs of a person which disturbs his balance. A person moves to fulfil his unsatisfied needs by conditioning his energies. There are dormant energies in a person, which are activated by channelising them into action.

2. Internal and external factors that stimulate desire and energy in people to be continually interested and committed to a job or subject or to make an effort to attain a goal.

3. Motivation results from the interaction of both conscious and unconscious factors such as (1) intensity of desire or need, (2) incentive or reward value of the goal and (3) expectations of the individual and of his peers. These factors are the reasons one has for behaving in a certain way. An example is a student that spends extra time for a test because he wants a better grade in the class.

Gives you a sense of personal satisfaction.

Goal Setting

Goals make your life more challenging, but at the same time, they give you a sense of personal satisfaction. Setting and reaching your personal goals help you appreciate your capabilities and give you an idea of your full potential.

Gives you a sense of purpose in life.

- After working for years, I have come to believe that each one of us is born with a unique life purpose. Identifying, acknowledging and honouring this purpose is perhaps the most important action that successful people take. They take the time to understand what they are here to do and then they pursue that with passion and enthusiasm.

- For some of us, our purpose and passion in life are obvious and clear. We are born with a set of talents and we develop our talent into skills through persistent practice.

Goals are incredible things. They provide direction and meaning to our lives. Goals provide us reason to live our lives. When you attain your goals, you find other reasons to live and the pursuit for a better life starts.

What are the benefits of goal setting? Anyway, you are probably the person who already makes a careful analysis of your conditions, set your goals and then marches ahead to attain them.

Perhaps, you agree that goal setting is a useful concept; however, you never have to look here and there for doing that. Perhaps it's still worse, you are just not able to see that there is no use investing time and effort for goal setting. Why are you worried? We feel one way to motivate yourself to set goals is to minutely think about the benefits of this activity. Here, to start with, we suggest you eight benefits of goal setting. Hopefully, they may accomplish three things. Firstly, they may help you to address the value of goal setting. Secondly, they may provide signals for you to take action. Lastly, they may help you attain your goals.

❑❑

8

Why Should You Write Down Your Goals?

In 1979, a group of researchers decided to conduct a goal-setting study on the Harvard Business School graduating class to assess how written and planned goals affected later outcomes in life.

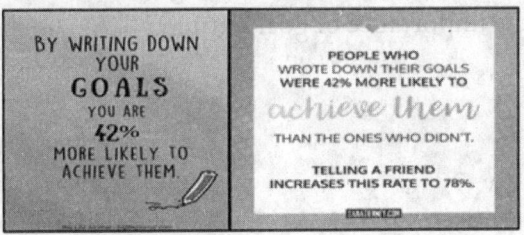

This Harvard MBA study on goal setting is referenced often on the Web but the details are usually obscure or confused. Since so many have made references to this study, I wanted to demystify and dispel any confusion surrounding the same. Often, people confuse this study with another often-talked-about study on the Web that was conducted in 1953 at Yale University.

This study was similar to the Harvard goal-setting study; however, back in 1996, Lawrence Tabak debunked that study in an article of Fast Company, where it was claimed that it had appeared in the middle of the best selling video of one of the world's most renowned motivational speakers, Zig Ziglar.

That study looks nearly identical to the Harvard MBA study. Tabak was unable to verify the Yale study after attempting to track the sources down. Not even Yale University itself was able to verify the study by researching its vast annals of information and literature.

So, did the 1953 Yale Study actually exist or was it simply concocted by motivational gurus to excite people about the importance of goal setting?

❏❏

9

Smart Tips for Goal Setting

SMART goals are:

- **Specific:** Well defined, clear and unambiguous.
- **Measurable:** With specific criteria that measure your progress toward accomplishment of your goal.

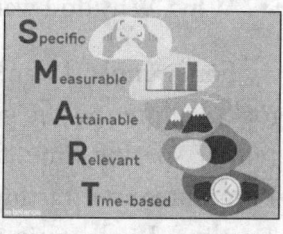

- **Achievable:** Attainable and not impossible to achieve.
- **Realistic:** Within reach, realistic and relevant to your life purpose.
- **Time Bound:** With a clearly defined timeline, including a starting date and a target date; the purpose is to create urgency.

SMART Goal

Specific

Goals that are specific have greater chance of being attained.

To make a goal specific, five 'W' questions should be considered.

- ❖ **Who:** Who is involved in this goal?
- ❖ **What:** What do I want to accomplish?
- ❖ **Where:** Where is this goal to be achieved?
- ❖ **When:** When do I want to achieve this goal?
- ❖ **Why:** Why do I want to achieve this goal?

For example, 'I want to get in shape' would be a general goal. A more specific goal would be "I will go to specific gym at specific time and will do workout everyday for 45 minutes and starting on 23 March 2020 with my 39" waistline, I will attain waistline of 36" by 23 September 2020."

Specific

Specific gym, specific physical measurements like waistline from 39" to 36".

Waistline from 39" to 36" means 1 inch every two months. This can be easily measured.

This is definitely achievable (Some people try to do from 39" to 29" - that is difficult and not easily achievable).

Achievable

We should first set the goal for 3" and after attaining the same, may set another goal stage for another 3".

Realistic

This is certainly realistic. As we have stated earlier, 39" to 29" in six months is not realistic; 3" in six months is realistic.

Timely

This is definitely time bound, as the person has decided to accomplish the goal by 23 September 2020.

SMART Goal: Measurable

A SMART goal must have criteria for measuring its progress. If there are no criteria, you will not be able to determine your progress and whether you are on track to reach your goal. To make a goal measurable, ask yourself:

1. How many/much?
2. How do I know if I have reached my goal?
3. What is my indicator of progress?

For example, building on the specific goal mentioned above:

I want to obtain a gym membership at my local community centre and work out for four days a week to remain healthy. I will aim to lose one pound of body fat every week.

SMART Goal: Achievable

A SMART goal must be achievable and attainable. This will help you figure out the ways for you to realise that goal and work towards the same. The achievability of the goal should be stretched to make you feel challenged. But it is well defined so that you may actually achieve it. Ask yourself:

1. Do I have the resources and capabilities to achieve the goal? If not, what am I missing?
2. Have others done it successfully?

SMART Goal: Realistic

A SMART goal must be realistic in that the goal can be realistically achieved given the available resources and time. A SMART goal is possibly realistic if you believe that it can be accomplished. Ask yourself:

1. Is the goal realistic and within reach?
2. Can time and resources be assigned to the goal?
3. Are you committed to achieve the gaol?

SMART Goal: Timely

A SMART goal must be time-bound in that it has a start date and an end date. If the goal is not time-constrained, there will be no sense of urgency and motivation to achieve the same. Ask yourself:

1. Does my goal have a deadline?
2. By when do you want to achieve your goal?

For example, building on the goal mentioned above:

On 1 August, I will obtain gym membership at my local community centre. In order to be healthy, I will work out four days a week. I will aim to lose one pound of my body fat every week. By end of August, I will have realised my goal if I lose four pounds of fat in a month.

The Importance of SMART Goal Setting

Often, individuals or businesses will set themselves up for failure by setting general and unrealistic goals such as "I want to be the best for X". The goal is vague with no sense of direction. SMART goals set you up for success by making goals specific, average, achievable, realistic and timely. The SMART method helps push you ahead, gives you sense of direction and helps you organise and reach your goals.

❏❏

10

Mercedes Story

Ramesh (imaginary name) is a person who knows the formula for SMART goals and wants to apply the same in his life. He wants to buy  a Mercedes in his lifetime. He went to the market and bought a poster of a Mercedes car that was a red coloured car. At home, he pasted the same on to a wall and wrote down the date 31 December 2020 (assumed) that was the date of purchase 30 months after 30 June 2018.

He believes the cost of the car is ₹36 lakh and he may save ₹90000 to ₹1 lakh every month. He may realise this dream easily in 36 months, but he can plan to attain the same in 30 months. Now, let's have a look at the formula of SMART goals.

He attained the goal of creating the fund of ₹36 lakh for buying the car by mid-December 2020. Now, he took the poster and went to the car showroom and said to the manager, 'I want to buy the same model of car in the same red colour on 31 December 2020. What would be the on-road price of that car on 31 December 2020?" The showroom manager told him that on-road price would be ₹36 lakh but the model in red colour was not available with them and he could choose some other colour. Ramesh replied, "I want that colour only." The showroom manager said, "If we order for the same colour, it would take at least 30 to 40 days and hence, he may arrange for delivery somewhere between 31 December to 15-20 January 2021."

Ramesh insisted that he wanted the model in the same colour and on the same date 31 December 2020 and he would not compromise on any thing. Ramesh wondered how could he convince the showroom manager that he was driving this car in his dreams for the last 30 months! How could he change the colour of the car now? And he was now convinced that the formula of SMART goals did work and the Almighty would surely find some way out.

Finally, the showroom owner said, "Saheb, I will need some time to look for this model in another showroom." And ultimately, Ramesh received a call from the showroom manager after few days, "Saheb, after a lot of effort, I am able to find the model with the same colour in another showroom, but there is some problem." Ramesh asked, "What's the issue?" The showroom manager said, "That is a display model. If you are interested, I can instruct them to shift the car from that showroom to our showroom." Ramesh told him that he did not have any problem with that. The showroom manager further informed that they would offer a discount of ₹6 lakh, as it was a display model. Ramesh accepted the same with inner happiness. Now Ramesh believes that the SMART goals formula does work 100 per cent. He feels when he has the plan to buy a car, he is capable of managing ₹30 lakh in 30 months. Now the same car is available at the same price. He is now feeling so happy.

Finally, that day of 31 December 2020 arrives. Ramesh goes to the showroom with the poster. Everybody in the showroom knows Ramesh's story by now. The owner Shri Dalip Wadhwa wants to meet Ramesh with that special model. Just when Ramesh enters the showroom and shows that poster to the manager again, Wadhwa arrives in the showroom to make the delivery. Shri Dalip Wadhwa gets tears in his eyes when he looks at the poster. Ramesh asks him the reason for his tears. Shri Dalip replies, "You are not only getting the car with the same colour but also getting the same car that you are showing in the poster because it is the same model that was used for photo shoot."

Lesson: This is the power of SMART goals formula.

Goals Push you Forward

Having a goal written down with a set date for accomplishment gives you something to plan and work for. A written goal is an external representation of your inner desires; it's a constant reminder of what you need to accomplish. There is a very common pattern that comes with working towards goals that we are all familiar with. You set your mind to something. You get excited and work like mad and then motivation starts to wane. Having goals that you can focus on and visualise helps you better connect yourself with your inner desires and gives you the motivational energy you need to work through periods where your focus inevitably starts to wane.

Goals help us. Setting goals for yourself is a way to fulfil your ambition.

Goal setting isn't just about creating a plan for your life and holding yourself accountable. It's about giving us the inspiration necessary for things we never thought of.

Do you want to accomplish something that many people dream about but few people ever accomplish? Unless you make it a goal for yourself and work everyday towards achieving it, why would you ever believe that you could accomplish the same? Unless you see yourself making progress slowly, your dreams and aspirations are nothing more than vague notions floating around in your imagination.

Goals Hold you Accountable for Failure?

If you don't write down concrete goals and give yourself time for achievement, how can you fail? And if you fail, you should re-evaluate your path. There is something quite humbling about looking back on a goal you have set for yourself 6 months, 1 year or 5 years ago and realising that you were supposed to accomplish a lot more than you actually did. It's a concrete sign that whatever you are doing is not working and you need to make real changes where you want to be.

Set Goals, what you Really Want?

There are certainly times when we set goals that don't really reflect what we really want. Sometimes we think we need more money when we really want a change of environment or someone to love. Sometimes we think that we want more of free time, but what we really want is work that we can be really passionate about. Sometimes we think we want to be alone but we really need to be close to more positive people.

If you don't set goals in the first place, how do you find out what you truly want? If you wander through life with vague notions of "success" and "accomplishment", you may never know that buying a new BMW will not bring you true happiness, or that landing that coveted promotion at work will make you unhappy because the extra money and fancy title won't be there for the reduced time with your family.

Ask yourselves what you really want and constantly re-assess your goals; we thus gain the benefit of introspection and self-reflection. We can figure out what it is we really want in life, and then we can go out and do it.

When you take the time to set goals, you ensure that your life is ready for getting the most out of every moment. There's so much to do and experience in life; but many of the things we want to achieve and experience are not handed over to us. We need to work for it.

Imagine you're on a vacation. You have a limited amount of time to take in all the sites, sounds, and experiences of a foreign land. Wouldn't you want to figure out exactly what you want to do and what you want to see? Or would you wander around, hoping to find something interesting? And if you do have some sites and landmarks in mind that you want to visit, wouldn't you do a little research to find out how to get there? Or would you wander around, hoping that you'll eventually find the place you're looking for?

In many ways, life is like a vacation (though it certainly doesn't feel like that). We have been given a finite amount of time to pursue the experiences we want. If you want to get out of the most precious moments of your life, you have to know what you want.

Of course, this doesn't mean you have to plan for every single moment of your life. After all, what's a vacation without a little seriousness?

During your journey, you'll find lots of interesting things to see and do that you never would have thought of before you started. This may result in change in your destination, as you travel down the road and learn more about yourself and the world you inhabit. But without a clear sense of what you want to do and where you want to go, you'll never be able to live life to the fullest.

Goals Allow You to Measure Progress

By setting goals for yourself you are able to measure your progress because you always have a fixed endpoint or benchmark to compare with. Take this scenario for example. David makes a goal to write a book with a minimum of 300 pages. He starts writing every day and works really hard; but along the way, he writes how many more pages he has written and how much more he needs to write. So rather than panicking, David simply counts the number of pages he has already written and he instantly determines his progress and knows how much further he needs to go.

Goals Lock You In Uncontrolled Situations

By setting goals you give yourself mental boundaries. When you have a certain endpoint in mind, you automatically stay away from certain distractions and stay focused towards the goal. This process happens automatically and subtly but happens as per research. To get a better idea, imagine this. Your best friend is going to Switzerland and his flight takes off at 9:00 PM. You leave your work after 8:30 PM to see him off and you know it's a 20-minute walk to get to the airport. So, you should make it a goal to reach the airport in 15 minutes by jogging so that you can have more time to say your goodbyes.

Would you get distracted by "anything" along the way? Would you stop for a break or a snack? Would you stop by your house before going to the airport? I am sure you answered each question and at the end of the day, this is what a goal gives you - focus. No matter which way you meet or what you see (nothing is normal), your goal allows you to stay locked in. You subconsciously keep away from distractions and your focus remains only on the goal. And by the way, if you still don't know how you become successful, you set a goal, you lock it in and then give it your 100%.

Goals Give You Motivation

Have you ever felt in your entire life that the root of all the motivation or inspiration is a goal? Goal setting provides you the foundation for your path. By making a goal, you give yourself a concrete endpoint and get excited about. It gives you something to focus on and put 100% of your

Find out a purpose to attain your goals.

effort. This focus is what develops motivation. Goals are simply tools to focus your energy in positive directions. These can be changed as your priorities change, new ones added, and others dropped.

What is the Purpose of your Goal?

A goal is something we strive for that should be aligned with our purpose. Goals are meant to do that. They serve our purpose. Our purpose does not serve our goals. It helps us create them. When you are rock-solid in your purpose, you can focus on the right things and get where you want to go.

It was his passion and an obsession in planting trees that led Jadav Molai Payeng to grow a thriving, lively 1360-acre forest near the river Majuli in Assam. The forest — larger than the central park in New York City — is now known as the 'Molai forest'. Payeng has earned the title "Forest Man of India".

For Payeng (now a Padmashri awardee), it all began at the age of 16, in 1979, when he encountered some dead snakes on a tree-less sandbar. He understood they were dead because they didn't have any shelter of plants or trees from the sun. He then decided to transform the place into a forest.

He set a goal to plant trees there. Keeping the wild animals alive was his purpose. He began planting bamboo seedlings on the sandbar. Same year when the social forestry division of Golaghat district launched a tree plantation project, Molai, who belonged to the Mising tribe (earlier called Miri) was hired as a labourer.

But when the five-year project had to be discontinued after three years, Molai continued looking after plants. Despite planting trees, other labourers abandoned the area. And for over three decades, no one noticed the obsession of that man. He cleared 10th class. He lived there with his wife Vinita and his children. He was rearing dozens of cows and buffaloes.

Molai's efforts came into knowledge of the forest department officials in 2008 when they were in search of a herd of 115 elephants responsible for damaging property in a nearby village. The herd had totally damaged their homes and the villagers were abusing them for the loss of their crop. But Molai was having one of the happiest days in his life, as he saw life, with the size of elephants, coming back to his forest. The large and dense forest was well appreciated by the officials. The world took notice of the man.

Now the Molai forest houses Bengal tigers, Indian rhinoceros and many variants of trees and plants. Now that Molai forest of 1360 acres is living its own life.

Look for a Purpose to Attain a Goal

When the number of people demanding computers and the number of companies manufacturing computers were on the rise, all the companies were taking interest in computer business to see that new companies were coming up in the market. There may be computers and some operating systems on different commands. The person who wants to work on computers undergoes a course on computer operations.

There was an operating system in the form of DOS. This was quite specialised and tough to work on. You need to remember commands to operate the system.

Around the same time, Bill Gates was trying to develop a new system that did not require an operator to remember its commands. All the commands were available on the click of a mouse.

Mercedes Story

Bill Gates was trying to solve the problem of an operator and eventually, he developed a software that did not require the operator to memorise the commands. All the commands are available on the click of a mouse. That software is WINDOWS.

Its purpose is to make the operating system simple. This is the main reason behind its success. If a person has a purpose in life to solve the problems of others, he would definitely make money. Suppose a person attempts to provide a solution for booking cabs. If the person gets ₹10 for every booking, he would make lot of money. Suppose he solves the problems of 1 crore users every month, he would earn ₹10 crore every month i.e., ₹120 crore every year. This is the power of purpose.

We may find a number of such examples in our life. OYO Rooms helps people book hotels through a mobile app and it is also making money. PAYTM is also the latest example. The person who helps people make payments through mobile is making money.

Purpose is an important part that helps you attain your goals. In your daily routine, you may pay attention to the examples of rich people and find out what they are doing by way of their products or services. You may easily discover

A GOAL WITHOUT A PLAN IS JUST A WISH

that every rich person is earning by solving problems of others. If you offer quality or you have the best price for solving a problem, this penchant for solving problems would definitely make money for you.

The Best Way to Plan Out Your Goals

If you want to start achieving your goals, you have to break them down into steps that don't completely stress you out. You will have to break your yearly goals into action steps and make them happen during the year.

Set goals for health, finance and business (more clients, products sales and sponsors etc.). From there, you will have to figure out what you need to do on a daily, weekly, and monthly basis to make them happen.

Goals should not be daunting. You simply need an achievable action plan, as it will help you achieve your goals. I'm talking about a simple process you can use to break down your goals into action steps. Keep reading the tips so you can create your own step-by-step goal plan.

Our goals can only be reached through a vehicle of a plan, in which we must fervently believe and upon which we must vigorously act. There is no other route to success.

– Pablo Picasso

What is an Action Plan?

An action plan is a step-by-step method to get things done. Among small and  more manageable people, it's a way to break up huge and heavy tasks. If you're overwhelmed by the amount of work your goal will take, an action plan will make it feel achievable.

Why do I need an Action Plan?

Creating action plans for your goals is something that breaking your goals down into an action plan helps you get more work done and generally you feel more on top of your life. Also, it's rewarding to feel that you are making progress. This takes you ahead towards achieving your goal.

Improve Your Habits to Achieve Your Goals

Identify a daily or weekly habit that will keep you on track with your goal. For example, keep your phone in airplane mode while you work. Habits are the framework for success, so it's important to align your habits with your goals.

Review Your Action List from Time to Time

Review your list of action steps and order them in a way that makes sense based on what needs to happen first. Review weekly or monthly progress, but review is necessary.

Visibility

Try to be clear on how you would write what you're going to write. Keep your goals in a visible place so that you see them often and you're reminded of the same. Review your goals every morning or every week as part of your routine.

Responsibility

Take responsibility for your own actions. You have an obligation towards yourself, so commit to yourself and your future. Don't blame others for delay in your success. Try to be consistent with your actions and make efforts day in and day out for attaining your goals.

Resiliency

If you get off track, pick up and keep going. There's no point wasting your energy by worrying about how far behind you are. You may have to adjust some deadlines here and there (or completely), and that's okay. Keep your vision alert for the pinnacle of your future. You'll find a way to get there.

Action-plan in Goals

"By thinking about your goals every morning, many times during the day and every night, you start moving towards them automatically."

– Bob Proctor

Benefits of Positive Thinking

We will now explain the power of positive thinking. We are sharing this with you, as there is lot of negativity in the market. When the market goes up, everybody becomes happy and when the market falls, everybody gets panicky. For those who maintain positive thinking in the market, it is a fact that the sketch on a stone is permanent, as a bearish trend is temporary whereas a bullish trend is permanent. You will have to maintain a positive attitude in the market in every case, as negativity would test your patience, prompt you to sell and harm you. Beware of negativity about the market. Always maintain a positive stance towards the market.

Here, you may understand positive thoughts about the market. And if you harbour negative thoughts about the market like it's a place of gambling, you should get rid of such thoughts and always have positive thoughts like it's a place to make money. This is the most important aspect of life and those who make money in the market are always positive about the same.

Positive Thinking

Stop negative self-talk to reduce stress.

Positive thinking helps in stress management and can even improve your health. Practice overcoming negative self-talk with the examples provided.

Is your glass half-empty or half-full? How do you answer this age-old question about positive thinking? Your outlook on life, your attitude toward yourself, and whether you're optimistic or pessimistic? It may even affect your health. Indeed, some studies show that personality traits such as optimism and pessimism may affect many areas of your health and well-being.

The positive thinking that usually comes with optimism is an important part of effective stress management and effective stress management is associated with many health benefits. If you tend to be pessimistic, don't despair. You can learn positive thinking skills.

Understanding Positive Thinking and Self-talk

Positive thinking doesn't mean that you keep your head in the sand and ignore life's less pleasant situations. Positive thinking just means that you approach unpleasantness in a more positive and productive way. You believe the best is going to happen, not the worst.

Mercedes Story

Positive thinking often starts with self-talk. Self-talk is the endless stream of random thoughts that run through your head. These automatic thoughts can be positive or negative. Some of your self-talk come from logic and reason. Other self-talk may arise from misconceptions that you create because of lack of information.

Example

Suppose a person is having headache.

For once, he feels that he would not go to office. Then, his mind would suggest him, "It would be better to stay back at home today and I would inform the office or the boss that I am not keeping well and I am not coming to office today."

Focusing on Positive Thinking

You can learn to turn negative thinking into positive thinking. The process is simple, but it does take time and practice. After all, you're creating a new habit. Here, some ways to think and behave that are more positive and optimistic.

❏❏

11

Benefits of Visualisation

Visualisation: Definition

The following are the minimum criteria that help in visualisation. Visualisation has the power of achieving dreams. A good  visualisation definitely means doing more; however, these criteria are useful for drawing a line in the middle of many things that are often referred to as visualisation and we reflect on visualisation in this field.

The purpose of a visualisation is to stimulate your mind. This means that data is something that is abstract or

Benefits of Visualisation

at least not visible immediately (e.g., inside human body). This controls photography and image processing with closed eyes. Visualisation makes invisible targets visible.

Building an image. It may look obvious that a scene has to produce an image, but this is not always so apparent. Besides this, a visual should be the first means of communication. Other modalities may only provide additional information. If image is only a small part of the process, it is not a visual.

The result should be readable and identifiable. The most important criterion is that visualisation should provide a way to learn something about data. Any alteration in non-trivial data of an image would leave the information; but at least some relevant aspects of the data would have to be studied. Visualisation also should be identifiable and it should not pretend to be something else.

The following example is found in the film 'Om Shanti Om'. Shahrukh Khan is sitting along with his friends and, holding a bottle in his hand, is imagining that everything would be ok one day.

And that day will come when he will be awarded.

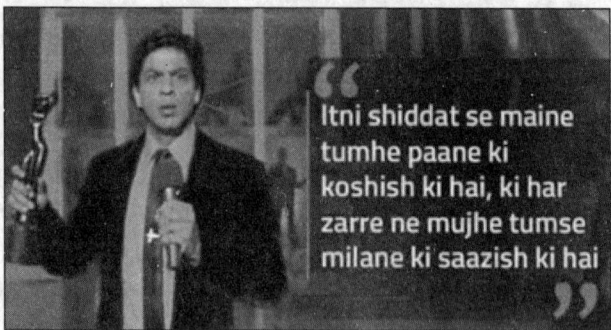

"Itni shiddat se maine tumhe paane ki koshish ki hai, ki har zarre ne mujhe tumse milane ki saazish ki hai"

You will have to imagine what you want to achieve in a stock market. What bank balance you expect from the stock market? You would have to visualise this on a daily basis what property you want to create from the stock market. We are passing through two instances during a day when we may indulge in imagination. The best time to awaken your imagination is morning and night. Morning, when we just get out of bed and the next time when we go to bed. We will have to visualise what we want from the stock market. We will discuss in detail about the action plan for stock market. We will have to develop a strategy for the stock market. First, we are trying to build your goal to be accomplished from the stock market, and then we have discussed your action plan.

We will discuss in detail about the action plan, like we have a frightening negativity about stock markets. We are trying to get rid of that negativity by means of various techniques and processes, like when we cook dal at home, we first of all remove dust and other particles that are not

Benefits of Visualisation

dal. In the end, after the filtering process, we go ahead with the cooking. This is a very important process before cooking.

We are trying to prepare our mind and brain for the stock market. Once you make up your mind for the stock market, we will tell you about the operations in the market. We will tell you how you may function in the stock market. When your mind is charged with positivity and you are able to visualise that you are making money in the market, you may certainly adopt the principles and processes that we will discuss for making money in the market.

Suppose you are making the mistake of typing 'end' in place of 'and'. Then, take a printout of wrong 'and' from the printer. If you use an eraser and make correction on paper repeatedly, and then you give a command to print again and assume that the error would be corrected, it's not possible. If you want to get a correct printout, you will have to make correction in computer itself; after that you will get a correct printout. That is what we are trying to convey that we will have to sharpen our mind before entering the market.

❏❏

12

Benefits of Stock Markets

Profitable Market

Let's come to the stock market now. You may start investing with a small amount of ₹5000 or ₹10000 and gain confidence of earning. Once an investor starts making profit on regular basis, he may plan for increasing his investment amount. End result - if you forget 'greed and fear and small returns', your returns would make trading profits amazing.

Many investors are dumbfounded - should they invest in stocks? Before taking a decision to invest, it is important to have a precise understanding of stocks instead of just accepting the common myths.

❖ Stock markets have fascinated people for over a century. Stocks are the fastest means of getting rich; however, there are in fact only a few investors who look at the stock market and stocks in right perspective. For the most of them, this is just price numbers that are going up and down. If your number goes up, you make money; if your number goes down, you lose money. This is both the beginning and the end of the story; but a thoughtful investor is more prudent. He not only views stocks as excerpts going up and down but also as real and live businesses in action. Take a step forward and realise that investment in stocks may be one of the best asset classes. That is a vehicle and mechanism that provides common individual investors some amazing profits and opportunities - profits that are unique among all the asset classes.

Scalable Business, That Does Not Involve Scalable Costs

What is Scalability?

Scalability is a characteristic of a system, model, or function that describes its capability to cope and perform well under an increased or expanding workload or scope. A system that scales well is able to maintain or even increase its level of performance or efficiency even as it is tested by larger operational demands.

In financial markets, scalability refers to financial institutions' ability to handle increased market demands. In the corporate environment, a scalable company is one that can maintain or improve profit margins while sales volume increases.

This concept is closely related to economies of scale, wherein certain companies are able to reduce their production costs and increase profitability, as they are big and produce more. For situations when increasing production increases costs and lowers profits, it is called 'diseconomies of scale'.

Understanding Scalability

Scalability, whether it is in a financial context or within a context of business strategy, describes a company's ability to grow without being hampered by its structure or available resources. The idea of scalability has become more and more relevant in recent years, as technology has made it easier to acquire companies, expand markets and scale.

Example of Scalability in the Technology Sector

For example, some tech companies have an amazing ability to create opportunities for high growth. The reasoning behind this is the lack of physical inventory and a software-a-service (SAS) model of producing goods and services.

Benefits of Stock Markets

Companies with low operating overhead and little burden of warehousing and inventory don't need a lot of resources or infrastructure to grow rapidly.

This is an amazing business that can be easily made a standard. There is no additional cost for making trading in stock markets easy or increasing this business.

◻◻

13

Portable Profession

Portable Profession Means

Small and totally or easily portable and not tied to electric wires.

- ❖ This can be operated anytime any where in the world using laptop or smartphone. This is the most portable profession in the world. No other profession can match its portability. This is such an amazing profession. You may practise this profession at home. You may practise this even at your office. You can practise this profession even while travelling. Not only that, even if you are out of your town or out of your country, you may still practise this profession easily. This profession just requires you to carry out two types of transactions - buy stocks or sell stocks.

It's quite easy to practise this profession with the help of laptop or smart phone. The apps provided by broking companies provide a lot of facilities. These apps have convenient options to buy or sell stocks. This is the most portable profession in the world.

No Additional Cost for a Startup

Definition: A startup company in its initial stages of the startup operations is enterprising venture that is generally aimed towards providing solution for a real-world issue through an innovative product or service.

❖ A startup is a company that is in the first stage of its operation. These companies are often initially controlled by their enterprising founders; this is because they try to raise money to develop their product or service that they believe is in good demand.

❖ Then, how do funding rounds work? Startups don't just raise a lump sum of cash but get a startup business loan and then be set up for life. Each of them is known as a 'funding round'. Each round is designed to give entrepreneurs and their business babies enough capital to get to the next milestone or stage.

❖ The promise of big, easy and fast money to build business ideas has inspired countless entrepreneurs to throw their hats in the ring to try and get their share and made their visions a reality.

❖ For some entrepreneurs, raising capital to build businesses and exit the bubbles has become a business of its own. Of course, in reality it is a little more complex and demanding than that. So, how do funding rounds work?

A startup company is a newly formed business with particular momentum behind it based on perceived demand for its product or service. The intention of a startup is to grow rapidly as a result of offering something that addresses a gap in a particular market.

There are no fixed parameters to define what kind of a company can be considered a startup, but the term frequently applies to high-tech companies creating products that leverage technology or perform some new task in a novel way.

Many startup companies don't have products for sale, and many do not have a revenue stream. In fact, when a startup is considered to be a startup, there are no firm rules. Some people suggest that a startup is such when it hits a certain size, completes its path to profitability, receives a high level of investment funds, becomes a public company or is acquired by a larger corporation.

Funding

The founders of a startup often lead the development of the product and serves as the organization's business leaders.

They often focus on scaling the company ahead for making profit. Facebook did not make a profit until 2009. Mark Zuckerberg founded the company after five years while he was a student at Harvard University.

As a result, the value assigned to a startup does not necessarily correspond with the actual revenue it generates during those early years. Instead, company leaders and investors might consider the company's potential value based on the profits it generates. Some founders bootstrap their young companies using their own financial assets - whether owned or borrowed - to fund their day-to-day operations. Others turn to angel investors when starting out, and later to venture capitalists.

Many work in incubators —workspaces and offices that are supported by non-profit or government organisations, as well as other institutions committed to developing these kinds of businesses. As such, these supporting entities often provide guiding leadership to seasoned business leaders and successful entrepreneurs.

Startup investors, along with the founders and other leaders within startups, often recoup their investments when they sell their startups to larger, more established companies. This is an exit strategy. Another strategy puts stress on making a startup public. Startups can also opt to stay private using their accumulated profits to reinvest in the enterprise and provide pay to the founders and employees.

There is no startup cost involved in equity market. This can be started with a small capital of ₹5000, just as Rakesh Jhunjhunwala had launched his career with ₹5000 and had earned ₹15,000 crores from the market.

No Additional Cost for Shifting

The 'Singur model' of industrialisation as represented by the now abandoned Tata Motors project in West Bengal has a number of regressive features. The Left Front government in West Bengal, in competition with other states for the location of Tata Motors' Nano automobile complex, fell overboard in offering subsidies to the company. Further, the government by offering highly fertile land in Singur, did not scrutinise the quantum of land demanded by the company and alleviated its mistake by invoking the Land Acquisition Act, thereby compelling landowners to surrender their land at a low price. Its compensation formula was biased in favour of non-cultivating absentee landowners, and unfair to the actual cultivators, bargadars and agricultural labourers, giving rise to opposition from peasants and their supporters.

After sit-down strike led by Mamta Banerjee, construction work for Singur factory of Tata Motors Limited started in August 2008 and an inconclusive talk was held between the Left Front government and the opposition. The Company decided to shift its plant to Gujarat. The opposition had not negotiated for this kind of consequence. The demand was made for restoration of

300-400 acres of acquired land to local peasants and the Company agreed to relocate ancillary producers to nearby areas and set up the plant in Singur.

Despite the plant set up nearing completion, the article wonders whether the plant would continue to be there? After securing a convincing victory in 2005 assembly elections on the back of its slogan of 'Development', leaders of the Left Front led by the Communist Party (Marxist) of India set out to invite big capitalists - both domestic and foreign, with fiscal incentives. They offered many other incentives with the hope of making West Bengal their preferred destination. This was seen as the only way to fulfil the aspirations of the people for jobs and prosperity. Soon after, the government claimed a great victory. Tata Motors Limited was persuaded to shift its 'revolutionary' small car project from Pant Nagar, Uttarakhand to Singur near Kolkata.

Besides the inherent technical and financial merit of the project, there was a general expectation that success of this project would bring along with it many other industries and projects and there would be manifold expansion in industrial production and jobs.

For some time, the car would be assembled and taken down from Tata Motors plant in Pant Nagar (Uttarakhand). This plant could produce 5000 Nano cars in a month (that was lower than the capacity of Singur plant). The sources revealed that it would take at least six months for the mother plant to get ready and shifting of the plant might result in a loss of ₹300 crores to ₹400 crores.

This is a story of shifting of a plant. There are many such examples where we encounter many challenges like sale of land and building, finding buyers etc. while shifting a plant. It's not easy to sell immovable properties overnight. This is a tough job. The bad part is that the buyers offer lower prices and do not get encouraged to buy immovable properties at current market prices. They want to make profit while buying lands and buildings.

Another challenge is to acquire building at the new place. If the location where you would like to operate is not available for sale, you would have to compromise on location etc. Shifting of the plant also involves a lot of expenditure. A lot of time is required to shift a plant. There would be heavy loss in production during the course of shifting. Suppose you are producing 10,000 cars in a day and shifting of the plant is expected to take 3 to 4 months. Just calculate assuming that a plant functions for 25 days in a month. Thus, you lose production of 2,50,000 units in a month and 10 lakh units in four months.

There is no shifting cost involved in the stock market. You may go ahead whenever you want to shift from one place to another. You may easily travel from one country to the other. There is no loss of even a single paisa in shifting.

Easily Manageable Profession

- ❖ There are many challenges for the management of a profession - uncertainty about future, financial management.

- ❖ There are many financial challenges in respect of business - timely payment to sellers, delay in payment to debtors, timely payment of salary, huge market credit, daily cash management etc.

Performance Monitoring

Every professional wants to increase his business. Many efforts are involved in maintaining and monitoring performance. Some undesirable events like demonetisation, implementation of new GST Act etc. may adversely impact performance.

Regulations and Compliance

In every profession, the person has to comply with many professional regulations. The problem is that many other challenges are facing compliance requirements. Many such compliance requirements are meant for getting back income tax, GST, Provident Fund Employees Insurance, corporation taxes etc. for business that not only fulfil all the compliances but also keep and maintain records related to official deficiencies.

Mobilisation of Merit and Right Talent

In a business, when the management selects a candidate, it knows whether he is a right candidate or an N.T. and whether it is investing a lot of money and time temporarily. Whether the person would stay with the business or not is always a great challenge. Only after a number of months, it gets to know that the person is not capable for the business and then it tries to replace him with a new candidate. This is a long process. This process involves many challenges. There is one more challenge - a right candidate leaves the production for any specific reason and the company is left with no option other than looking for a new person. This is a complete circle that the company encounters regularly.

Technology

Another challenge in a profession is substantial changes in technology. In today's world, we can see that technology is undergoing change every day. Technology is another challenge for a businessman. It's costly to adopt a new technology. For example, we may look at many recent changes - one of them is television. Many of the companies have disappeared because of their inability to adopt new technology. We have seen how television was initially in black and white format and later it underwent considerable development, like colour television, LCD, LED etc.

As we know, new technology involves a lot of investment and what's necessary for the old equipment only is - residual value. Another example is that of mobile phone where we have seen lot of transformation. New technology is also changing very fast, almost on daily basis. Customers demand new technology every day. Everybody would have to adopt this with fresh investment. There is no alternative to new technology and it's challenging to accept this.

Search for Data
- ❖ Customer Service
- ❖ Labour Management
- ❖ HR Policies.

Easily Transferable Business

Transfer of shares refers to the voluntary act of transmission of shares by one party to the other. Transmission of shares means - transfer of titles to shares by the operation of law by a deliberate act of affected parties - insolvency, death, inheritance. A share transmission is the process of transfer of existing shares by one person to another person - either by sale or as a gift. The shares owned by a person may be given away to another person as a gift.

Shares are considered 'movable property; hence it is not mandatory to execute a gift deed. However, it can be gifted. A gift is transmission of movable or immovable property from one to another without consideration. Shares owned by a person can be gifted to another person (relative or otherwise) by following a certain procedure. Since gifting constitutes a transfer, and the transfer is without consideration, such a transfer can be carried out using 'off market transfer' mechanism.

Delivery Instruction Slip (DIS)

Donor of shares has to fill out a DIS and submit the same to Depository Participant (DP). It should mention the DP ID, DP name, client ID and name, ISIN, and number of shares to be transferred. Execution date should be mentioned. This is an instruction to the DP.

The receipt instruction has to fill out a receipt instruction and submit the same to his DP. The shares received from the donor's DP will be credited to DP's account once the receipt instruction is received. Details such as DP ID and name are required to be mentioned.

Process

Once the DIS or receipt instructions are received, duplicate copies are returned to respective parties. Delivery instruction and receipt instruction must have referred details.

Point to Note:

* Once a gift is made, it is not revocable.

Portable Profession

Enjoyable Profession

This is the most enjoyable profession. When you understand how to invest in  the market and how to make money there, you feel a sense of joy. You know the system and you are earning income. Your money works for you here.

Supporting Profession

This also is a supporting profession. Suppose you know how to invest in the market and you are making money in the market; you will then help others to make money in the market. If you do something for others, you become a donor and the Universe in a way opens the door for you and provides you whatever you are giving to others.

Freedom from Office

You have the freedom to build or not to build an office for this profession. You will have to make investment as and when you want using your mobile or laptop and you will not need to open an office and maintain employees. It may be ok if you have brokership for a company or you have any other activity related to the stock market, otherwise you don't need to open an office. You will have to just use your mobile or laptop whenever you wish to buy or sell stocks.

Freedom of Time

You have freedom of time in this profession. You don't have to attend an office and work for the whole day. You have freedom to work - you can work as and when you wish.

There are two kinds of work, like study and pick up stocks. You can do this anytime. If you wish to trade in stocks or buy or sell stocks, you can do that anytime during market timings.

Freedom from Employees

You have freedom from employees in this profession. You don't need employees and you also don't have to make salary payments. Appointing and managing staff is also a major challenge.

Freedom of Products

In this profession, you have freedom not to manufacture any product. The company that you have invested in is primarily engaged in manufacturing products. You only have to monitor the stock and performance of the company. You are free to manufacture any product.

Freedom from Service

In this profession, you have freedom not to provide any kind of service to others. The company you have invested in is primarily engaged in providing services. You only have to monitor the stock and performance of the company. You are free to provide any service to anybody.

Business Partnership

In this profession, whenever you buy shares of a company, it means you become an owner of that company to the extent of the shares held by you. Till the time you have ownership of the shares, you have the ownership of that company also. Suppose you are buying a share of XYZ Ltd. This means that you are entering into a partnership of that company. When large investors invest in business, their hold and partnership in the same grow gradually.

Cash-only Business

This is a cash-only trade. This means you get payment in your bank when you sell stocks. These transactions are executed under the supervision of  depository, exchange and brokers. This is a cash-only business. Nobody would say that he would make payment after a week or a month. Other businesses involve lot of credits. This is a cash-only business.

Entry Any Time

You may enter this profession any time at any age. You may easily buy stocks any time you wish. Of course, opening of Demat account requires minimum age of 18 years.

Exit Any Time

You may exit this profession any time. There is no need of any specific time to exit the market. Whenever you want to exit the market, you just sell all your stocks and exit the market. You need a lot of time to exit in the case of other professions. Suppose you have set up a factory and you want to exit out of the same; you will have to find a buyer. Selling a property is another big job for anybody. It's a tough job to find a buyer for a property and selling plant and machinery is also a daunting task. Recovering money from debtors is a tough job and you also need to ensure official compliance that involves many challenges.

No Need of Market Credit

You don't need credit in this profession. Other businesses require lot of credits. Once you sell your stocks, the exchange and the broker take care of your payment and the amount is credited into your bank account directly.

No Credit Period

You don't need any credit period in this profession. Other businesses require lot of credit periods. Credit periods generally range from one week to three months. I have seen many cases where businesses are enjoying a credit period of six months. The situation is very grim in other businesses. Once you sell your stocks, the exchange and the broker take care of your payment and the amount is credited into your bank account directly.

No Credit Risk

This profession does not involve any credit risk. In other professions, when a businessman provides credit, there is some possibility of that payment not being made on time. In this profession, there is no possibility of loss of your payment. The exchange and the broker take care of your payment and the amount is credited into your bank account directly.

No Need to Look for Buyers

You don't need to look for buyers in this profession. This is a great profession where the exchange finds buyers for you. Once you decide to sell your stocks and issue instructions, the exchange presents the buyers and executes the trade for the buyer(s) at the price quoted by you. In other professions, a lot of effort is required to find buyers and then, you have to negotiate for the price at which you want to sell your product or service. This is a wonderful profession.

No Need to Look for Sellers

You don't need to look for sellers also in this profession. This is a great profession where the exchange finds sellers for you. Once you decide to buy stocks and issue instructions, the exchange presents the sellers and executes the trade for the seller(s) at the price quoted by you.

Generally, the buyer offers the market price. In other professions, a lot of effort is required to find sellers and then, you have to negotiate for the price at which you want to buy the product or service. This is a quite tough part of every profession. Finding sellers is a challenging task in any profession; however, there is nothing like that here. This is a wonderful profession.

No Risk of Volume Buying/Selling

This profession does not involve any risk of volume buying and selling. Nobody knows what you are doing when you buy stocks in volume. All these transactions are done online and payments are transferred directly from banks. In other professions, if you indulge in volume trading, it becomes a big challenge to transfer goods, as the same requires multiple meetings and lot of time. This profession does not have any such risk.

This Can Be Started with Minimum Capital

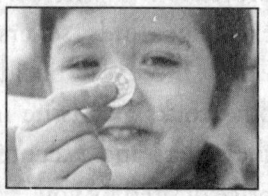

You may start this profession with a capital of just ₹100 or ₹1000 or whatever you want. Please tell me if there is any other profession that can be started with a capital of ₹100.

No Risk and No Loss

This profession does not involve any risk or loss. Other businesses have plenty of challenges for  minimising risk and loss. Suppose, for various reasons, AirTel Company is facing huge loss and wants to close its operations. Stopping a business is not easy. Every business has some worth in the market. Once the news about closure of your business spreads around, nobody would release your payments. The credits in the market would be withheld by the debtors.

No Fraud with Demat Account

The possibility of fraud or forgery in this profession is nil. The stocks are in Demat form after purchase. You would have only one instance of stock in your  Demat account and once your sell the same, it gets reflected in the other party's Demat account. Nobody can say he would not part with the stock. This is a 100% foolproof system. There is no possibility of fraudulence.

No Government Compliance

❖ Like Income Tax, GST, PF/ESI etc.

❖ Government compliance in this profession is rare. Other businesses involve a number of government compliances like Income Tax, Sales Tax, Provident Fund, Employee State Insurance and many others. This is quite a cumbersome process for a while. In this profession, there is no government compliance requirement other than short term capital gains and long term capital gains. This is a profession where you have to follow very few rules.

No Record Keeping and Paper Work

There is no need to maintain any record in this profession. Other professions require maintenance of various records like Income Tax, Sales Tax and other records. There are many professional account managers for maintenance of records. Here, your Demat account provided by your service provider would take care of records. All your records are there in your Demat account.

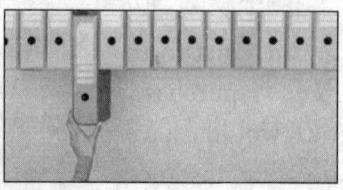

Business in Autopilot Mode

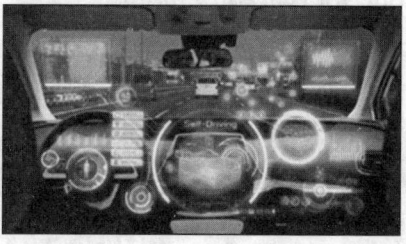

I have observed that many businessmen want their business to run in autopilot mode. This is a nice idea for any business. Presently, we may find plenty of books and videos that provide solutions for running your business. There is demand in the market and hence, there are many trainers and coaches who provide training for running business in autopilot mode.

They are charging you lakhs of rupees for training you in such techniques. No doubt this is a nice technique and I am not claiming that it is wrong. This is an autopilot mode profession. You don't work for the whole day. I have explained many points that you don't need to employ anybody for this and you don't have to work more than an hour on daily basis. This is enough to operate in this market. Once you become an expert and invest your capital, you wouldn't need to work 8 to 10 hours a day. Just work for an hour per day for analysis and trading. After that, you will have to work on quarterly basis to maintain that portfolio. Two to three hours per quarter is enough to operate in the market. Suppose you want to identify some stocks for your investment; we will provide you some principles that definitely work and you would be able to find out the stocks by spending just a few hours.

This happens once in a while and you would need this just once or twice in a month.

After understanding the benefits of stock markets, you may easily realise that this is an amazing profession of the world. No other profession in the world can match its benefits. The business of stock markets is a big business. I have not seen so many benefits in any other profession. Some businessmen are fighting to secure credits, some are struggling with the manpower while some others are facing a number of challenges for complying with various government departments' requirements.

Because of the existence of challenges and so many businesses of the stock market, we need to properly understand the challenges only. In India, many people are incurring loss in the market, as they are not conversant with the market. They don't know how to create income and make money in the stock market. As much as possible, we are trying to explain how to operate in the market and how to become multimillionaires and billionaires using stock markets.

Combating Global Pandemic Corona, COVID (19/2020)

The entire world is facing a global pandemic COVID (19/2020) in 2020. All the businesses have stopped. Every country and state had lockdown conditions. Everybody was facing a dangerous situation. Everybody was confined to his/her home and going out was prohibited. This virus had gripped almost all the countries and many people were already infected.

None of the businesses were operational at that time. All the businesses, factories, offices and shops were closed; however, the only place where people were making money was the stock market. The investors who knew how to make money in the stock market were earning by working only for some time using their laptop/mobile at home. The market was providing the investors a number of opportunities and the investors who understood the market were taking advantage of those opportunities.

Money Saving Tips

Birthday/Wedding Anniversary

We celebrate at least four birthdays in a year in our family. On various occasions, try to invest some amount 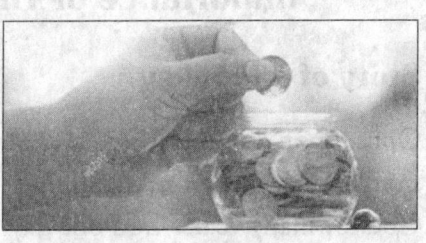 in stock market also. We feel if we have a budget of ₹10000 for the birthdays of our children, we should restrict the same to ₹5000 and be ready to invest the rest ₹5000 in stock market. If we are able to save ₹5000 on every birthday, we can save ₹20000 in a year and we may invest that amount in stock market. We may also save ₹5000 on wedding anniversary. Thus, you are able to save ₹25,000.

Annual Travel Expenses

We all visit our friends and relatives during vacations every year. As we know, this entails a lot of expenses. What we can do here is that we may only make short travels within India and save money for investment. Assume we have a budget of ₹50000; we will have to save at least ₹10000 out of our travel budget and invest the same in stock market. This will give you good return and will also build your wealth and your financial future.

Importance of Time Story

Story of a Monkey

Once upon a time, there was a monkey. He kept on worshiping God for many years. God one day appeared before him and asked the monkey, "What do you want?" The monkey replied, "I want to be a prince." God said, "Ok, but there

is a condition. Four days from today, you would see full moon in the sky for a moment. At that very moment, you go to a tree and jump into the pond that is just under the tree. You will then surely turn into a prince."

God's words made the monkey quite happy. He went to other monkeys and narrated the entire story to them. All the monkeys were quite happy to listen to the same. The day arrived when the monkey was to turn into a prince. All the monkeys climbed to the tree together and waited for the right moment. The monkey who had to look up in the sky, was waiting for the moment when it would be full moon.

That moment arrived after some time and the moon was in its full shape. At that very moment, that monkey jumped into the pond. All other monkeys were waiting for the moment when the monkey would come out as a prince; they were also wondering whether this was actually going to happen. When that monkey actually turned into a prince, all the other monkeys also jumped into the pond.

None of the other monkeys turned into a prince after the moment had passed

Lesson: There is a right moment to enter and exit the stock market. If you wait for others, you may lose money or miss the chance to make money.

Fundamental Analysis

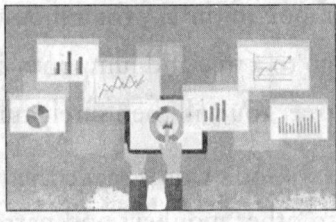

Fundamental analysis is a vast subject. A separate book is required to provide all details on the subject. In the future, we will write a book on fundamental analysis only for the people who wish to study this further. Here, we will cover the subject in brief to enable everybody to understand the same and easily make money in stock markets.

We will have to first of all, explain fundamental analysis. We will include only important points in this chapter. We will talk about fundamental analysis in brief. This is a vast subject and if we try to explain in detail, it may take the form of a book or this book may get quite lengthy. We will cover this analysis in brief that would be comfortable for anybody to understand.

Fundamental analysis is a very important step for choosing the right stocks. If we perform a fundamental analysis for every company, we would be always winner. We need to have a deep understanding of fundamental analysis before making investments. Fundamental analysis is the backbone of stock market.

A lot of details are required for fundamental analysis. If we want to understand this fully, we may have to write another book for the same. If investors wish to study this further, I would write another book on fundamental analysis. Once you go through a book, some things become clear to you while some things remain obscure. Generally, a common investor wants to understand the basic things for working with the stock market.

A number of ideas and principles have been presented in respect of stock markets. I believe too many things generally confuse investors. A habit of reading is not common in India. We have seen most of the famous books originating in developed countries. If people in India develop their habit of reading further, they may add more value to their lives. Many writers in India have authored great books on various subjects, but only few of them are well known. Not a single book out of them is inspiring for making real money in the stock market. We present necessary details to help you understand fundamental analysis; this would help everybody to make money in stock markets.

There are several websites relating to stock markets. We believe in bseindia.com as this is the official website of Bombay Stock Exchange that makes available quite authentic and original data provided by the companies. Other websites may have minor variations based on date and information may prove to be wrong.

There are many kinds of originality; however, this is the age of information technology and we possess mobiles and laptops and we are comfortable with all these as we work with them. This is the reason that we have explained the points with websites, as this is a very effective way in current times. We are providing fundamental analysis in proper procedure to suit the users. This is the most appropriate advertising effective system for analysis of fundamental principles. We are trying to explain the terms that we generally use in our daily life. Some information is provided only for awareness. For analysis of the basic things, we will cover the most important parts that you will need to use in all cases.

The following screen gets displayed when you open bseindia.com website.

Everybody uses mobile and laptop in this computer age. Our generation uses mobiles. People want to do everything with mobiles; hence, we will explain this as per laptops or mobiles. As we are now using technology, we must introduce the common words that we see on the screen.

Previous Close

Previous close is a security's closing price on the preceding time period of the one being referenced. Previous close almost always refers to the prior day's final price of a security when the market officially closes for the day.

Opening Price

The opening price is the price at which a security first trades upon the opening of an exchange on a trading day. For example, the Bombay Stock Exchange (BSE) opens at 9:15 am.

High

'High' is the highest price during a specific period. 'Low' means the lowest price during a specific period. 'Long' is basically when you think a stock is going up, and you are having shares of the company.

Low

Low means the lowest price during a specific period. Long is basically when you think a stock is going up, and you are having shares of the company. Short is when you are thinking a security will go down, so you bet against the security.

Highest

Highest means the highest price during a specific period. 'Low' means the lowest price during a specific period. 'Long' is basically when you think a stock is going up, and you are having shares of the company. 'Low' means the lowest price during a specific period. 'Short' is when you are thinking a security will go down, so you bet against the security.

52-week High

52-week High is the highest price at which the share has traded during the last one year. This is a technical indicator used by some traders and investors who view this figure as an important factor in the analysis of a stock's current value and as predictor of its future price movement.

52-week Low

A 52-week Low is the lowest price at which the share has traded during last one year. This is a technical indicator used by some traders and investors who view this figure as an important factor in the analysis of a stock's current value and as predictor of its future price movement.

Upper Price Band

An upper price band is a value-setting method in which a seller indicates an upper and lower cost limit, between which buyers are able to place bids. The price band's floor and cap provide guidance to the buyers. This kind of auction is called price-determination technique. This also prevents major rise and fall of the specific stock. The upper price band also prevents the price of the specific stock to move beyond that level. This is a basic surveillance system.

Lower Price Band

A lower price band is a value-setting method in which a seller indicates an upper and lower cost limit, between which buyers are able to place bids. The price band's floor and cap provide guidance to the buyers. This kind of auction is called price-determination technique. This also prevents major rise and fall of the specific stock. The lower price band also prevents the price of the specific stock to move below that level. This is a basic surveillance system.

2-week Average Volume

A 2-week Average Volume for a stock is the average number of the stock traded per day during 2-week period. Daily volume is the number of stocks traded per day, but two-week period is used to arrive at the average volume. You may observe that the volume may vary considerably on any particular day. If you find the variation to be significant, you should analyse the same in detail. This is good indicator to find out whether the stock is popular. If the volume is large and the price is going up, it means that somebody is trying to buy the same in bulk. This may attract a good price or it may be a 'dump and pump' attempt. If the stock is fundamentally strong, it is a good sign to buy and if the stock is fundamentally weak, this is an opportunity for 'pump and dump'.

What is 'Pump and Dump'?

'Pump and Dump' (P&D) is a type of securities when somebody wants to commit a fraud where the price of a stock owned by him is artificially inflated through false, misleading and exaggerated statements so as to sell the stock at a high price. The public finds the stock rising and buys the same with the hope of a good return. In fact, he gets trapped and ends up incurring heavy loss.

TTQ

Sum total of all the shares of a particular company, bought and sold in a particular session, is referred to as 'Total Traded Quantity' (TTQ).

Trade (CR) - Share Turnover

This is a measure of stock liquidity calculated by dividing the total number of shares traded over a period by average number of shares. The higher the share turnover, the more liquid company shares are.

M Cap Full (Cr)

'Free Float Methodology' is a method of calculating the market capitalisation of an index's underlying companies. 'Free Float Methodology' market capitalisation is calculated by multiplying the equity's price with the number of shares readily available in the market.

M Cap FF (Cr)

Market Cap Free Float is a free float methodology that is used to calculate the market capitalisation of an index's underlying companies. 'Free Float Methodology' market capitalisation is calculated by multiplying the equity's price with the number of shares readily available in the market. This means that the share is free to trade on any specific day.

Record Price

The cumulative record price of total shares of any company represents its statutory capital that the corporate is bound to maintain. Only funds over and above that can be issued to investors as dividends. In short, funds that cover the face value in a way work as a kind of default reserve.

EPS (TTM) - Earning Per Share (Trailing Twelve Months)

Earning Per Share (TTM) is calculated by dividing total earnings or profits of a company by the total number of outstanding shares. Earnings Per Share is usually abbreviated as EPS and TTM that follows stands for Trailing Twelve Months.

PE - Price to Earnings Ratio

'Price to Earnings Ratio' is the ratio of a company's current share earnings. This indicates the return expectations of the market. This also indicates how much importance the stock is receiving in the market. How to define PE? PE ratio is a simple calculation - current share price divided by earnings per share (total earnings during last 12 months divided by the number of outstanding shares).

PB - Price to Book ratio

Price to Book Ratio compares a company's market value to its book value. The market value of a company is its share price multiplied by the number of outstanding shares. Price to Book Value Ratio is calculated by dividing the market price per share by the book value per share. Per share market price is simply the stock price. Per share book value is the company's assets adjusted against debts divided by the number of shares.

Return on Equity (ROE)

This is a measure of profitability that calculates how much profit a company generates relative to its total amount of shareholders equity. The formula for ROE is -

ROE = Net Income / Shareholders' Equity.

ROE is also sometimes referred to as Return on Net Worth.

Class

In respect of financial markets, category refers to asset classes where investors may invest. There are different categories of instruments for investment, like debt instruments, equity instruments and portfolio having both.

When we open the stock market website of bseindia.com and look for a stock, we may check whether the stock is listed under stock category.

Group

Out of all the stocks listed on BSE, those in 'A' Group are the most liquid. Market rate makes Group A stocks the best in all aspects and they exhibit comparatively higher volumes. There are Group B and Group C also.

List

S&P BSE Sensex Heat Map is a great tool to track S&P BSE SENSEX stocks. The index is widely reported in domestic and international markets through print media. Beta measures the sensitivity of a Securities Price movement relative to the movement in the S&P BSE Sensex.

Industry

'Industry' is a sector of economy in which businesses are primarily engaged in producing finished goods and services. This may also be understood as an industry or market that shares common operational features. Dividing an economy into different sectors permits more intensive analysis of the overall shape of economy.

Currently, there are three kinds of industry - Extraction of Raw Materials (Primary), Manufacturing (Secondary) and Services (Tertiary). They have been further sub-divided into many sectors; for example, under manufacturing, automobile, auto parts, domestic appliances etc.

Now, let's understand the basics of left side block on bseindia.com screen.

Equity

It displays different elements on this tab. This is on the main screen. You may get the stock graph in this and may view the pattern of graph for a desired period; some of them we have discussed earlier.

Derivatives

There is one more tab below Equity tab where you may view call and put options and various other derivatives as dropdowns.

SLB (Securities Lending and Borrowing)

Securities Lending and Borrowing

Securities Lending and Borrowing describes a market practice whereby securities are temporarily transferred from one party (the lender) to another (the borrower) via an approved intermediary.

The borrower is obliged to return them either on demand or at the end of an agreed term and also has an option to return early. The lender may recall securities at any time within normal market settlement cycle.

SLB is a major and growing activity that provides significant benefits for issuers, investors and traders alike. SLB helps in improving market liquidity, more efficient settlement, tighter dealer prices and reduction in the cost of capital.

Why Participate in Securities Lending & Borrowing?

Lender's Motivation

It provides lender incremental return on an idle portfolio.

Borrower's Motivation

- To cover a short position, avoidance of settlement failure
- Hedging of futures and options positions
- Borrow and lend to reap the benefits of market sentiment

Corporate Announcements

This is the tab that is very useful to get the latest news about a company. On this tab, you may check the latest news and company's future events and various other details through dropdowns.

Financials

This is one of the most important parts of fundamental analysis.

The above screen displays quarterly returns. There are two tabs here. They are—Quarterly Trends and Annual

Trends. This is one of the most important screens and we will check the most significant part of fundamental analysis in this.

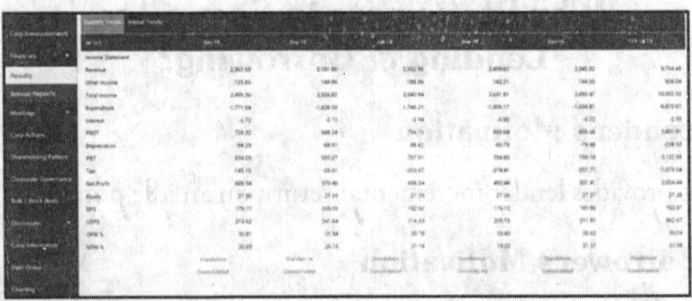

There are four things that you need to analyse carefully.

1. Revenue

Firstly, we will have to investigate the quarterly revenue. This should be always moving upward. Hence, we will have to check this carefully before making investment. There are three kinds of companies that are growing. If revenue is going up, it indicates that the company's profits and business are growing and the company's management is capable of developing the business and is quite effective in managing the business. Hence, it is suggested to invest in such companies.

Maintaining

We may also find that some companies are not growing in terms of revenue, but they are able to maintain their business as per previous years. This means that these companies lack something compared to the companies that are growing their businesses. It's not suggested to invest in such companies.

Decreasing

Their revenues are on decreasing trend. This clearly indicates that the management of such a company or its conditions are not capable of developing or maintaining the business. Hence, it's not suggested to invest in such companies.

2. Interest

This is also the most important part of fundamental analysis. This reflects the amount of interest paid by the company in a quarter. If we want to check annual interest, we will have to multiply the quarterly interest by four. This indicates the extent of borrowings. Eventually, this impacts net profit.

If the company is listed, it indicates that it is capable of taking money on interest from its shareholders. If the company is able to mobilise capital from shareholders without interest, it will have to pay interest on bank loans that are availed on interest. A good company or management always endeavours to reduce bank borrowings.

In this analysis, you will have to investigate the interest part - either low or minimal, and if the company is not trying to pay back its borrowings, the interest component would get reduced in every quarter. If interest amount has come down, this is good and appropriate for investment. If interest is not increasing, it may still be considered for investment. And if the company is increasing the interest component, it indicates that the company is going for fresh bank borrowings resulting in increase in quarterly interest. Hence, it's not suggested to invest in such a company.

3. Net Profit

Increasing

If net profit is increasing, it indicates that the company has the capacity to increase profits. This means that the management is efficient and it has the strategy to increase profits. Such companies are good for investment.

Maintaining

We may also observe that some companies are not showing growth in net profit, but they are maintaining the level of business as per previous years. This means that these companies are falling behind the companies that are growing their business. It's not recommended to invest in such companies, as the industry wants development only.

Decreasing

These companies show reducing net profits. This clearly means that the management or the condition of the company is not capable of developing and maintaining the business. Hence, it's not recommended to invest in such companies.

4. NPM Percentage (Net Profit Margin)

NPM or Net Profit Margin is the profit margin of a company. There are three kinds of profit of a company; they may be subdivided as below:

- ❖ 10% - 15% NPM
- ❖ 15% - 20% NPM
- ❖ Over 20% NPM

It's recommended to invest in companies that have NPM of over 20%, as the companies that have high profit margin would make good profits and that in turn would benefit their investors. First of all, we need to decide the sector in which we wish to invest, and then we will have to check NPM of all the companies in that specific sector; we will then be able to find in that sector the leading companies that are capable of achieving maximum NPM of that sector. It's recommended to invest in such companies.

In some cases, NPMs of the companies in a specific sector range between 10%-15% NPM and 15%-20% NPM. That indicates that the entire sector has a low margin. After that, we will have to find out the company that has the maximum NPM in that sector. That means, you will have to invest in the company that maintains good NPM in its own sector. You will then be linked to the best company in the sector and there will be greater chances of good returns.

Once we decide to invest in a company, we will have to look into and monitor the same and analyse its results on a quarterly basis. We will have to definitely spare some time for analysis of quarterly results of the company. If the performance of the company is not good, we will have to investigate the same deeply and analyse its reasons to understand whether the condition is same for the entire economy. Or, if the company has some other valid reasons, we may invest in the same, else we will have to invest in some other company that is performing well in that sector.

Example

Recently, we observed in March 2020 that Corona virus had become a global issue. The entire economy was struggling at that time and lockdowns were being enforced. The performance of that quarter was impacted at global level.

The above screen displays results on annual basis, but it is recommended to look at the quarterly results only. If we look at the annual results, we may recollect the events that have taken place during four quarters. And, if we review the results after full year, it is possible that the share price and the performance of the company might have come down by then. Hence, it is recommended to monitor only the results and development should not be limited to a quarter or a year.

Meetings

This is the tab that provides information on the meetings organised by the company and their results. This is a very effective way to find out the decisions taken by the company and then we may plan investments accordingly.

Corporate Actions

On this tab, we may view general actions taken by the managements and the corporates. This may include distribution of dividend or bonus on a previous date.

Shareholding Pattern

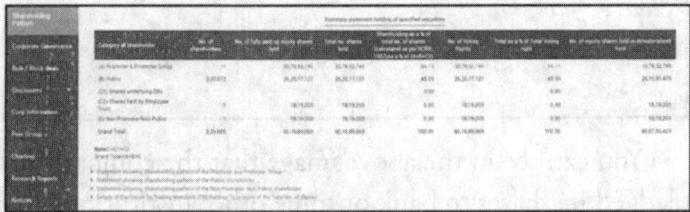

This is one of the most intense parts of fundamental analysis. The most important aspect of the same, that we need to verify, is that the promoters should have more than 50% stake. In the above screen, you can see that the promoter's shareholding is 56.15%, which is more than

50%. This means that promoters have their rights secured in the company. This means that promoters have their control over the company.

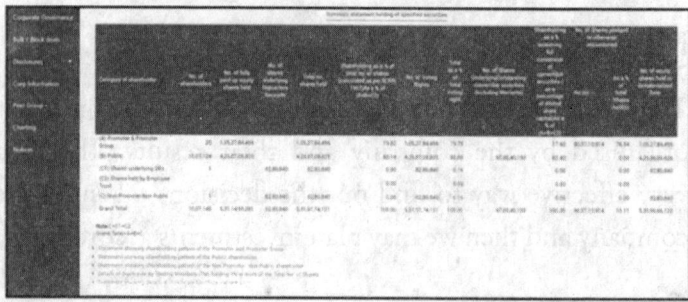

In the above screen, you can see that the promoters' holding is just 19.82%, which is less than 50%. This means that the promoters are losing their hold on the company.

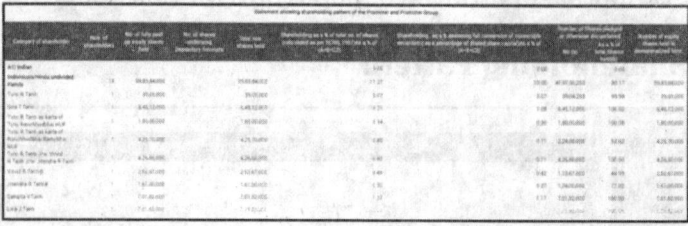

You can see in the above image that the company has pledged its shares to bank or some other institution. This means that promoters of the company have raised funds by pledging their shares. This shows that the management is not reliable as it is not capable to maintain and manage its promoters' stake and also that the promoters are not able to preserve holding of their shares.

[Table showing shareholding pattern of the Promoter and Promoter Group]

In the above image, you can see that the company has not pledged its shares to any bank or other institution. This kind of company is good for investment.

We suggest that promoters should have more that 50% shareholding and all their shares should be free hold and not pledged to any institution.

Corporate Governance

We can view corporate data of the company under this, like members and board of directors of the company, their dates of appointment and tenure etc.

Bulk/Block Deals

This tab displays bulk/block deals that other companies have made in this specific company. Here, you can see the names of such companies and their investments.

Disclosures

Under this, you can check the basic disclosures that the company has made in respect of its commitments, SAST, date of insider trading etc. This may be quite useful for analysing future prospects of the company.

Corporate Information

Under this, you can find the name and related details of the company, like its directors, promoters and their designations. You may also get their addresses and contact details on this tab.

Peer Group

This tab is quite important. Here, you can see all other companies that work in the same sector. Here, you may get an idea of all other companies that may be direct competitors of your chosen company.

Charting

This is the tab where you can see the company on charts. On clicking here, you will be redirected to a new tab where you can review charts for analysing the company.

Notices

This tab contains common notices issued by the company. These may be further downloaded and may also be seen in PDF format.

14

Market Capitalisation

What is Market Capitalisation?

Market capitalisation refers to the total market value of a company's outstanding shares of stock. This is commonly referred to as "market cap". It is calculated by multiplying the total number of a company's outstanding shares by the current market price of one share. As an example, a company with 10 lakh shares selling for ₹100 each would have a market cap of ₹10 crores. The investment community uses this figure to determine a company's size.

Generally, there are three types of companies in the market:

❖ Small Cap

- Mod Cap, and
- Large Cap

Basically, we will have to beware of the company having low market cap - ₹200 crores. Don't invest in such companies.

1. **Small Cap:** A small cap company is generally the one with market capitalisation between USD 30 crores and USD 2 billion i.e., ₹200 crores and ₹14000 crores (approx.).

2. **Mid Cap:** Generally, companies with market capitalisation between USD 2 billion and USD 10 billion i.e., ₹7000 crores and ₹70,000 crores (approx.) are defined as mid cap companies.

3. **Large Cap:** Generally, companies with market capitalisation above USD 10 billion i.e., ₹70,000 crores (approx.) are defined as large cap companies.

Intrinsic Value

Intrinsic value is also the most important part of fundamental analysis. First of all, we will have to check all the basic criteria of a company. If we find the company is good for investment, you will have to measure the intrinsic value of its share; then we will have to check the current price of the stock and then we will have to verify the book value of that specific stock to check if the value of the stock as compared to its book value is good or bad. As we have explained earlier, the book value of a stock means that the specific company has sold all its assets and disposed off its debtors. It will then be divided by the number of shares.

$$V* = \frac{EPS \times (8.5 + 2g) \times 4.4}{Y}$$

V: Intrinsic Value
EPS: the company's last 12-month earnings per share
8.5: the constant represents the appropriate P-E ratio for a no-growth company as proposed by Graham
g: the company's long-term (five years) earnings growth estimate
4.4: the average yield of high-grade corporate bonds in 1962, when this model was introduced
Y: the current yield on AAA corporate bonds

For example, book value of ₹100 for a company against an intrinsic value of ₹80 means that the stock is well priced and we should invest in that company. If in other case, the price of the stock is more, we will have to wait for a good book value or we will have to decide to look for another stock.

Summary

1. Revenue should Increase

This should be always going up. Hence, we should check this carefully before making investment.

Quarterly Revenue is Increasing

Check if quarterly revenue is increasing. If revenue is going up, it indicates that the profit and business of the company is growing and the management of the company is competent to develop its business and quite effective to manage the business. Hence, it's recommended to invest in such companies.

2. Interest

This is the most important part of fundamental analysis. Under this, we find out the quantum of interest being paid by the company in a quarter. This reflects the extent of borrowings. Eventually, this impacts the net profit. A good company and management always endeavour to keep bank borrowings to the minimum, thereby reducing interest. In this analysis, you have to verify that the interest is quite low or minimum and it's good if the company is able to reduce interest amount every quarter.

If the interest component goes down, it's good and appropriate for investment. However, if the company's balance sheet reflects increasing interest amounts, it means that the company is going for repeated bank borrowings. It's not recommended to invest in such companies.

Net Profit Should be Growing

A growing net profit indicates that the company has the capability to increase its profits. This shows that the management is efficient and it has the strategy to improve profits. Such companies are good for investment.

NPM Percentage

NPM should be more than 20%.

Market Capitalisation

Investment has been recommended in companies that have NPM of more than 20%, as the company having a high profit margin would make good profits resulting in good returns for its investors.

Choose the Company that is Leader in that Sector

First of all, we need to decide the sector in which we want to invest and then we will have to verify NPM of all the companies in that specific sector. We will then be able to identify the leading company that is able to achieve the highest NPM in that sector. It's recommended to invest in such companies.

Shareholding Pattern

This is one of the most intense parts of fundamental analysis. The most important aspect that we need to check is that the promoters should have stake of more than 50% and you should also check whether their holding is encumbered. Look into both the aspects carefully.

15

Technical Analysis

Technical analysis is also quite effective for investing in stock markets. Technical analysis would provide you signals for entry into a stock and exit from a stock. Technical analysis is a means for interpreting and predicting price movements in financial markets using historical price charts and market data. This is a foundation.

A businessman can interpret past market pattern. They can make very accurate prediction of future price projection curve.

Fundamental Analysis

Fundamental analysis is a method of measuring a security's intrinsic value by examining related economic and financial factors. The main objective is to arrive at the figure that an investor can compare against the current price of a security to check whether the security is rightly priced or 'overvalued'. This is one of the two stages of market analysis. Fundamental analysis is focused on the 'right price' of an asset. Technical analysis primarily using both interpretation of external factors and intrinsic value is purely based on price charts of the stocks. This is entirely identification of the pattern on a chart that is used for prediction of future movements.

However, technical analysis is an analytical approach for forecasting trends in price. One part of this technique is focused on the point how and why a technical analysis could work.

Technical analysis is a research into demand and supply of investment on the basis of historical trade information in terms of both price and volume. Technical analysis, often called chartists, believe that it is possible to detect the onset of a movement in stock or market value from one equilibrium condition to another. They use previous stock charts for this and for identifying trends, they use market movements that they believe would predict pricing movements. Chartists are not worried about why conditions are changing. They just want to identify the onset of a change in order to exploit the same for short term and medium term gains; though most of these analysts predict short term and medium term pricing trends, some of them also forecast long term market cycles based on their data.

Like many professionals in the security industry, chartists believe that the value of the market is determined by supply and demand for stocks. Besides this, chartists, like others, think that supply and demand are impacted by many factors and they are not always logical that may be measured by the market constantly and subjectively. Technical analysis is different from other schools of security forecasting; however, chartists believe that in times of stock price movements, stocks move in trends lasting over long periods and if they begin trend for the first time, investors can profit from such trends.

This supposition is based on two beliefs. First, chartists contend that information about stocks leaks into the market over extended period. Stock prices move gradually as information moves from the industry insiders to analysts and finally to investors. Second, chartists believe that a further time lag occurs because investors do not unanimously agree about the validity of the information or its impact upon the securities. The gradual nature of price changes gives investors time to act for taking advantage of a trend.

Thus, it is the job of the technical analyst to develop a system that can detect the start of a movement from one equilibrium price to a new higher or lower price. It should be underscored that chartists are too concerned with detecting the onset of a change in the supply and demand of a stock (or other investment) so that they can benefit from price changes associated with finding a new equilibrium.

History & Background

Technical analysis is, perhaps, the oldest form of security analysis. It is believed that the first technical analysis was conducted in 17th century in Japan, where analysts used charts to plot price changes in rice. In fact, many present-day Japanese analysts still rely on technical analysis to forecast prices in their stock exchange, which is the second largest in the world. In the United States of America, technical analysis has been used for more than 100 years. This form of analysis was especially helpful at the turn of the century when financial statements were not commonly available to investors.

In recent years, the ever-increasing use of personal computers has led to substantial growth in technical analysis, and numerous software packages have been developed to meet these increased needs. Thus, technical analysis can be applied not only to stocks and their markets but also to bonds, commodities, fixed-income markets, industries within markets, and currencies. Besides this, one of the most popular current applications of technical analysis is for futures derivatives.

Trading Rules

Technical analysts rely on many rules, often using several together when deciding whether to buy, sell, or do nothing with an investment. Some of the best-known rules are contrary opinion rules, rules that follow sophisticated investors, and rules that follow the market prices and volume. However, with other types of forecasting, these rules can be interpreted in a variety of ways, thus leading a variety of forecasts using the same information.

The first type, contrary opinion rules, maintains that the majority of investors are incorrect about stock decisions most of the time, but especially at market highs. Thus, when the majority of investors are very bearish, a chartist using this rule would say that it is a good time to buy; conversely, when the investor is bullish, this rule would dictate that selling is the best course of action.

In addition to using some of the above rules, chartists often take into account stock prices and trading volume when making their purchasing decisions. The Dow theory asserts that stock prices move in three different fashions:

(1) **Longer-term trends:** Any price movement that occurs over a significant period, often one year to three or five years. It's difficult to predict long-term trends and they are often constrained by brief changes against trends. The impact will be short-lived and then you may notice; however, you will have to examine long-term trends for long-term investments.

(2) **Short-run Movements:** Intermediate trend or mid-term trend - a common movement in price performance of securities that may extend from three weeks to six months. The analysts would examine cyclical behaviour of security to explain this.

(3) **Profit and Short-run Movements:** Short-term trend - a movement in price of an asset during a period of few hours to days. Day traders and technical analysts try to profit from short-term trends.

When analysing stock prices, chartists try to make out which way the long-term pricing trends are heading, realising that there will be short-lived trends in the opposite direction. In addition to having an interest in stock price changes, chartists are also interested in stocks' trading volumes relative to their normal trading volumes; whereas, a change in stock price indicates the net effect of trading activity, it does not give any information on how widespread the public interest is about the stock. Thus, if a stock price increases in an environment of heavy trading and then it has a setback in lighter trading, chartists would probably view it as a bull trend in stock, thinking that only a few investors were selling to make a profit.

Technical analysts also use the breadth of market measure to influence their decisions. This is a measure that compares the increase in price of stocks against numbers, the numbers that have decreased and the numbers that have remained stable.

Disadvantages, As Stated Earlier

Technical analysts make decisions with regard to cause of those trends by examining market and security trends. On the contrary, fundamental analysts have taken their decisions by relying on accurate information about companies and markets before it becomes available to the general public. Because technical analysts believe that it is possible to receive and process this information quickly. Many of the advantages relating to technical analysis correspond directly with the disadvantages of fundamental analysis.

For example, to project risks and future returns, fundamental analysts depend heavily on financial statements for information on a company's or industry's past performance. Technical analysts can forecast the future of a movement. Hence, technical analysis can work only when security markets are in some way inefficient. However, more recent studies suggest that small benefits can be polished with more complex technical trading rules; still, past pricing patterns are not always repeated in the future.

A forecasting technique can work for a time but later recollect a major market turn. Another disadvantage of technical analysis is that pricing forecasts can predict self-fulfilment. Thus, if a prediction is made about increase in stock price when it passes a given price, it will sometimes do so absolutely; because people will buy the stock at the threshold price giving hope for that increase to continue. In this situation, the stock price typically returns to its real equilibrium price at a later time.

A final problem is that there is a great deal of subjective judgment involved in making predictions. Two analysts can look at the same pricing history and arrive at quite different pricing projections.

'Technical analysis' is a method of forecasting security prices by examining past price movements and other obvious indicators of market activity. This technique rejects the more conventional mode of fundamental valuation based on financial statements. 'Technical analysis' also requires a lack of efficiency in the pricing process; however, many studies indicate that major security markets are too many, even if not fully efficient.

Price: High & Low

According to economists, this principle works everywhere in the market. This means that the stock prices change because of supply and demand. If more people want to buy a stock (demand)  than sell it (supply), the price goes up. Conversely, if more people want to sell the stock than buy it, there would be greater supply than demand and the price would fall.

Any trend is the normal direction of market price. Stocks in all markets get upgraded or downgraded. Data also have trends, like price traffic go up or down for a month.

Major Types of Trends

1. Bull Trend

What is a Bull Market?

- ❖ A bull market is the condition of a financial market in which prices are rising or are expected to rise in future. The term "bull market" is most often used to refer to the stock market; however, it can be applied to anything that is traded, as prices of stocks rise and fall essentially during trading. The term "bull market" is going to last for months or years.

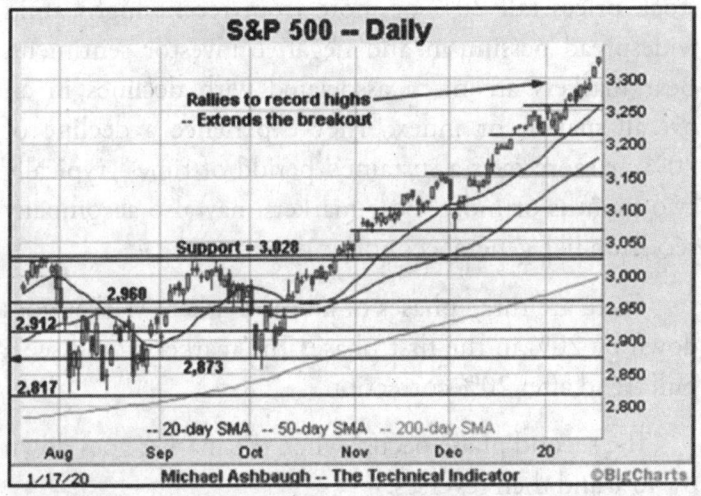

2. Bear Trend

What is a Bear Market?

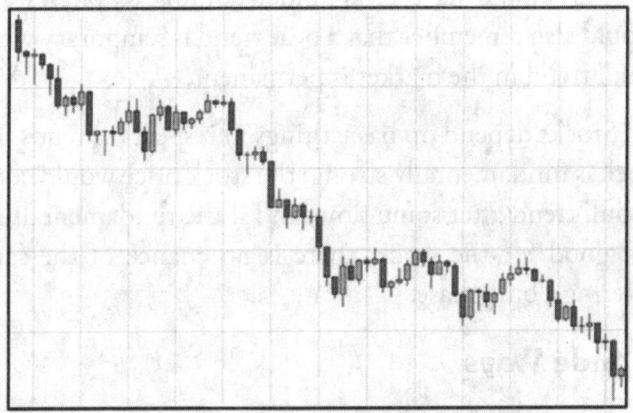

A bear market is when a market experiences prolonged price declines. It typically describes a condition in which stock prices fall 20% or more from recent highs amid widespread pessimism and negative investor sentiment. Bear markets are often associated with declines in an overall market or index. They experience a decline of 20% or more over a sustained period of time—typically two months or more. Bear markets may also accompany recession like general economic downturns.

There are three phases of a bear market. Market goes down by 20% in the first phase. The market would see a bull trend after 20% correction.

The second phase occurs when the market goes down by 40% and then reverses.

In the third phase, the market would go down by 60% and then reverse.

You should have clear understanding of phases and should also remember that a bear trend is temporary while a bull trend in the market is permanent.

Stocks depend on basic things in respect of trends. If a stock is fundamentally strong, the stock price would come in bull trend after some time, and if the fundamentals are not good for the stock, there is no chance of the same entering a bull phase.

3. Side Ways

A market is in sideways when prices of investments remain within a tight range for any period. They don't make higher highs or breakout above the previous highest price. A sideways trend often refers to the stock market. The small investor would make profit this time, as he knows the limits of the stock. When the stock falls below that and when it touches the high level, he would sell the stock and book profits. Ideally this is good when the stock breaks the support.

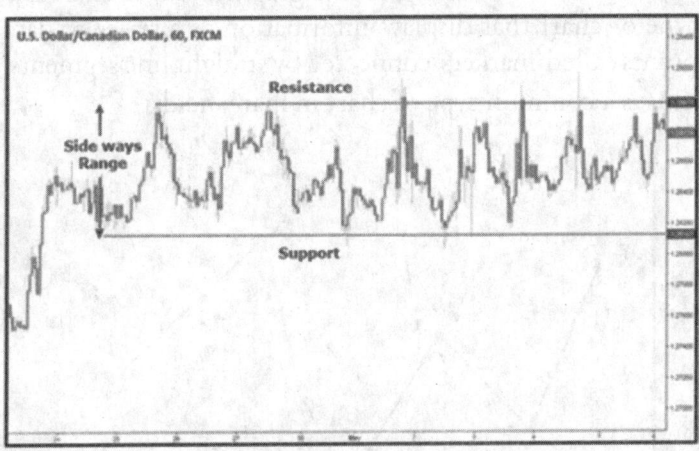

4. Trend Reversal

A trend reversal occurs when the direction of a stock changes and moves back in the opposite direction - downtrend reversing to uptrend or vice-versa.

- ❖ This is a good sign for investment in stocks. Generally, there is good scope for profit. You also wait for such movements.
- ❖ Chart/Graph Types

1. Line chart
2. Open High Low Close (OHLC)
3. Candle Stick chart

Line Chart

A line chart or line plot or line graph or curve chart is a type of chart that displays information as a series of data points called 'markers' connected by straight line segments. This is a common type of chart in many fields.

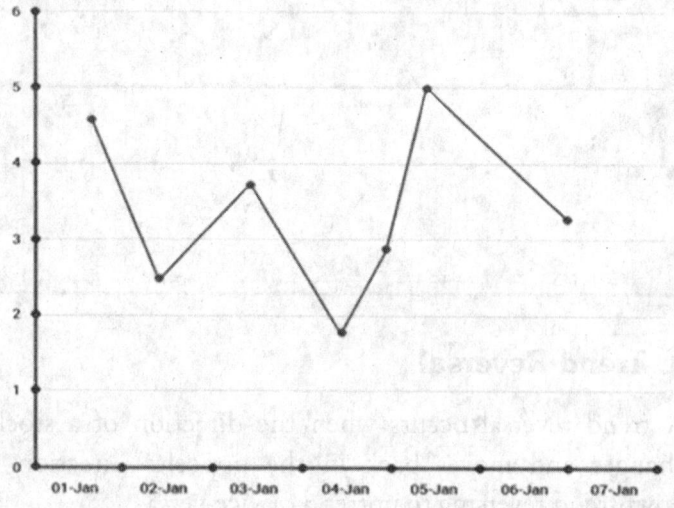

Line graphs are useful. They depict data changes and trends very clearly and may help in forecasting data results that have not been recorded yet. They can also be used for displaying many dependable variables against one independent change.

OHLC (Open High Low Close)

An OHLC chart is a type of bar chart that displays open, high, low and close price for every period. OHLC charts are useful as they show for a single period four data points out of which, close price is treated as the most important by many traders.

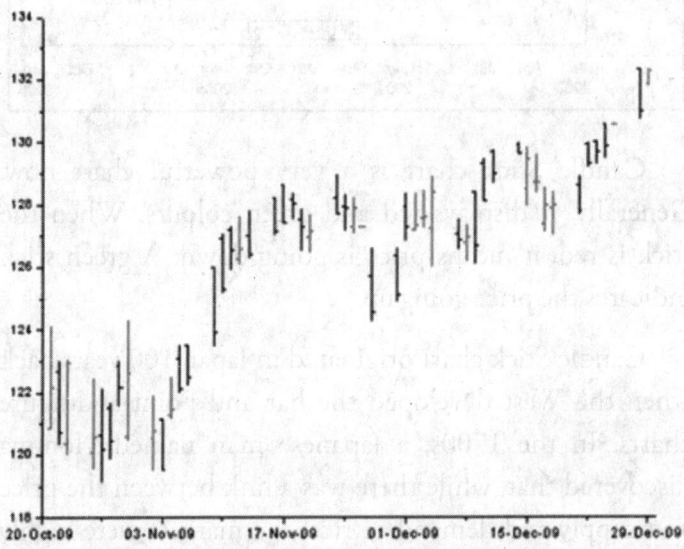

OHLC charts are useful as they show for a single period four data points out of which, close price is treated as the most important by many traders. This type of chart is useful as this can depict up and down movements.

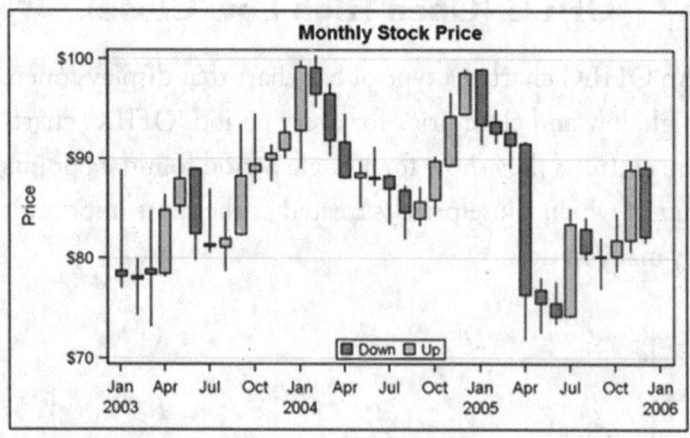

Candle Stick chart is a very powerful chart now. Generally, it displays red and green colours. When the stick is red, it means price is going down. A green stick indicates the price going up.

Candle Stick chart originated in Japan 100 years back when the West developed the bar and point-and-figure charts. In the 1700s, a Japanese man named Homma discovered that, while there was a link between the price and supply and demand of rice, the markets were highly influenced by the emotions of traders.

Candle Stick charts show that emotion by blindly representing the size of moves with different colours. Traders use the Candle Stick charts to make trading decisions based on regularly occurring patterns that help in forecasting short-term direction of the price.

- Candle Stick charts are used by traders to determine possible price movements based on past patterns. Candle Stick charts are useful. The traders specify when they trade. They show four price points (open, close, high and low) during that period.
- Many algorithms are based on the common price information shown in Candle Stick charts.
- Trading is often dictated by emotions that can be read in Candle Stick charts.

Benefits of Candle Stick Charts

- Determine current status of the market in a single view.
- View the market trend more easily.
- Identify market patterns quickly.

Candle Stick charts have many analysis components. We are here providing some instruments that are quite effective and you may use them while making investments.

Bullish Candle

- Bullish Candle: I make bullish a pattern when Close is more than Open (usually green). Bearish Candle: When Close is less than Open (red).
- A bullish pattern may be observed after a downward trend and may indicate opposite to a price movement. They are signals for traders to consider opening long positions.

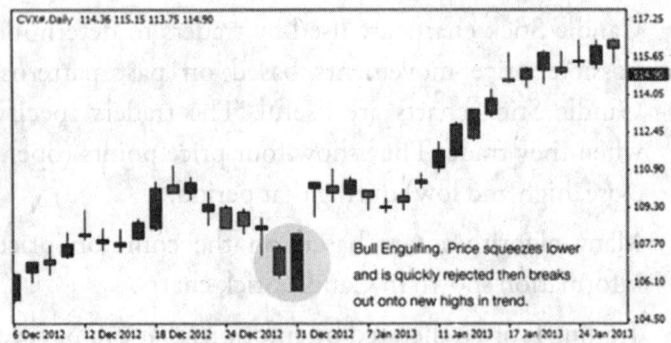

Bearish Candle

A bearish engulfing pattern is a technical chart pattern that signals lower prices to come. The pattern consists of an up (green) candlestick followed by a large (red) candlestick that eclipses or engulfs the smaller candle.

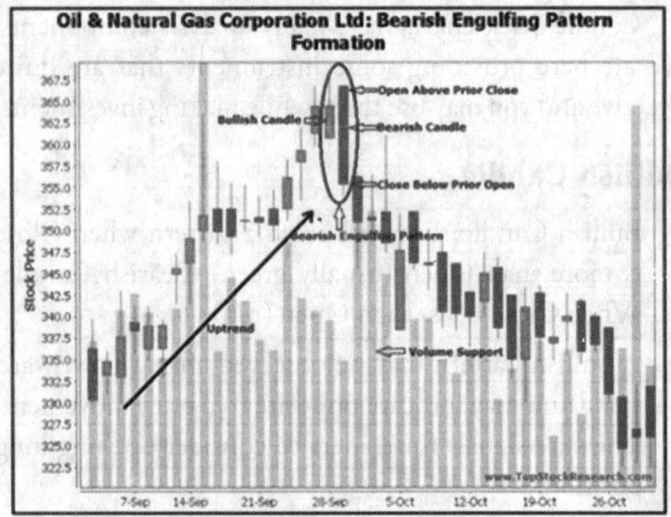

❖ A bearish pattern may be observed after an uptrend and may signal opposite to the price movement. They are signals for traders to consider opening short positions.

Doji

A doji is the name of a session, in which the candlestick for a security has an Open and a Close that are almost equal and often components in pattern. Doji candlestick looks like a cross, inverted cross or plus sign. Alone, dojis are neutral patterns that have also been featured in a number of important patterns.

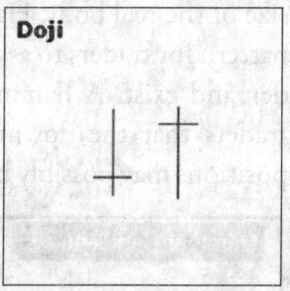

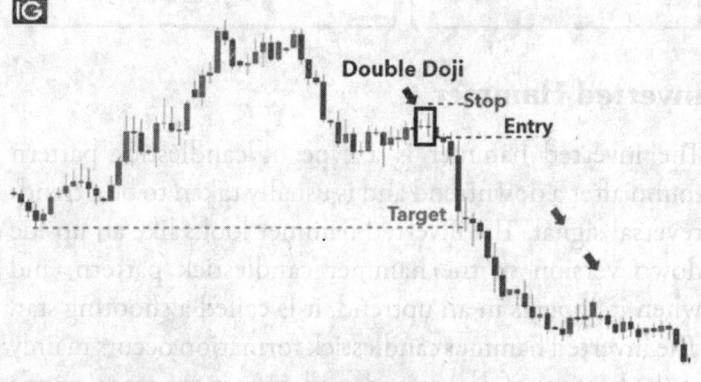

Hammer

A hammer is a price pattern in candlestick charting that occurs when a security is significantly lower than its opening but rallies within the period to come close to the opening price. This pattern forms a hammer-shaped candlestick in which the lower shadow is at least twice the size of the real body. Hammer is a very useful candlestick pattern for traders to assist them to see where support and demand exist. A hammer after a downtrend may signal traders that the downtrend is likely to end and short positions may possibly be covered.

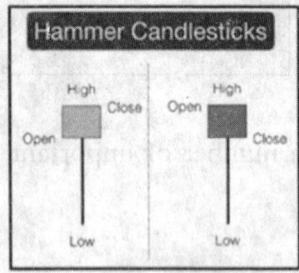 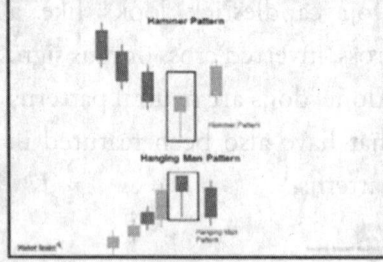

Inverted Hammer

The inverted hammer is a type of candlestick pattern found after a downtrend and is usually taken to be a trend-reversal signal. The inverted hammer looks like an upside down version of the hammer candlestick pattern, and when it appears in an uptrend, it is called a shooting star. The inverted hammer candlestick formation occurs mainly at the bottom of downtrends and can act as a warning of a potential reversal. It is important to note that the inverted pattern is a warning of potential price change for buying, not a signal by itself.

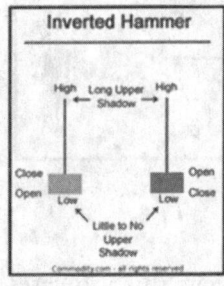 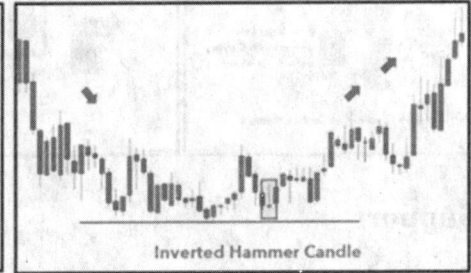

Bearish Harami

A bearish harami is a Japanese candlestick pattern that suggests price may soon reverse. The pattern consists of a long white candle followed by a small black candle. The opening and closing price of the second candle must be contained within the body of the first candle.

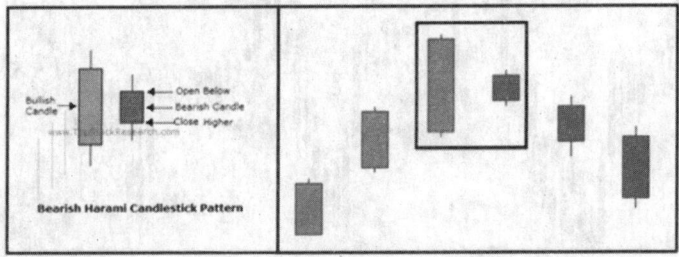

Bullish Harami

A bullish harami pattern is a basic candlestick chart pattern that indicates that the bearish trend in the market may reverse.

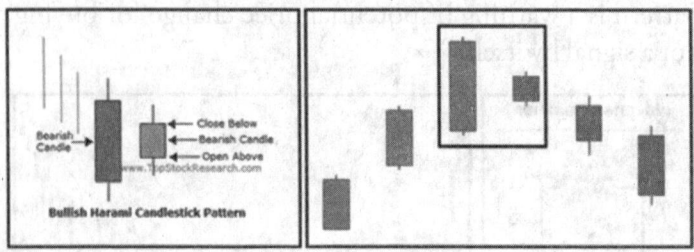

Support

One of the most important charts to view, this indicates that buyers are ending their inactivity and starting to buy stocks again. You should get this single candle when it is near a support level. This kind of level is often defined as moving average that acts as a moving support level during an uptrend.

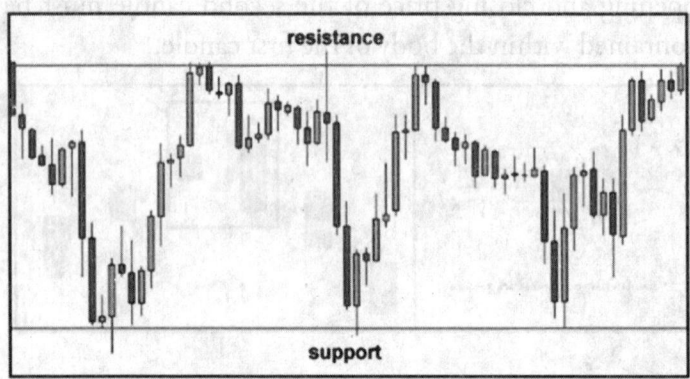

Resistance

One of the most important charts to view, the concepts of resistance are undoubtedly two of the most highly discussed attributes of technical analysis. Technical analysts use resistance levels to identify price points on a chart where probabilities favour a pause or reversal of the prevailing trend. This indicates that buyers are coming out of their inactivity and starting to buy stocks again. You should get this single candle when this is near a resistance level. This kind of level is often defined as moving average that acts as a moving resistance level during an uptrend. Hence, it's suggested not to go for investments for long period.

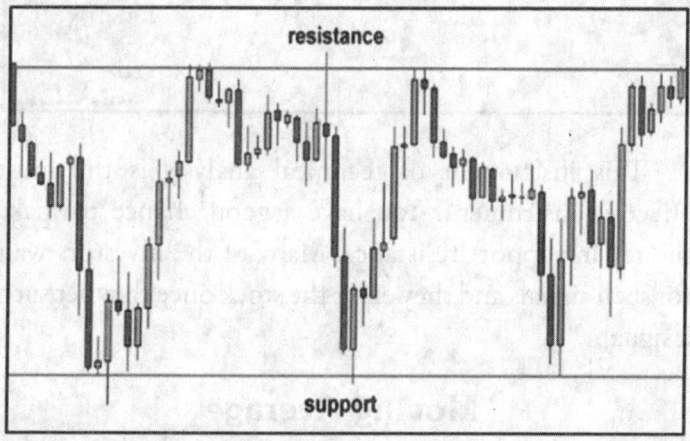

Resistance Breakout

This stage is known as Resistance Breakout. You will have to be very careful for this kind of signals. These signals would give you great profits. Be careful, you will have to also examine basic facts while entering stocks.

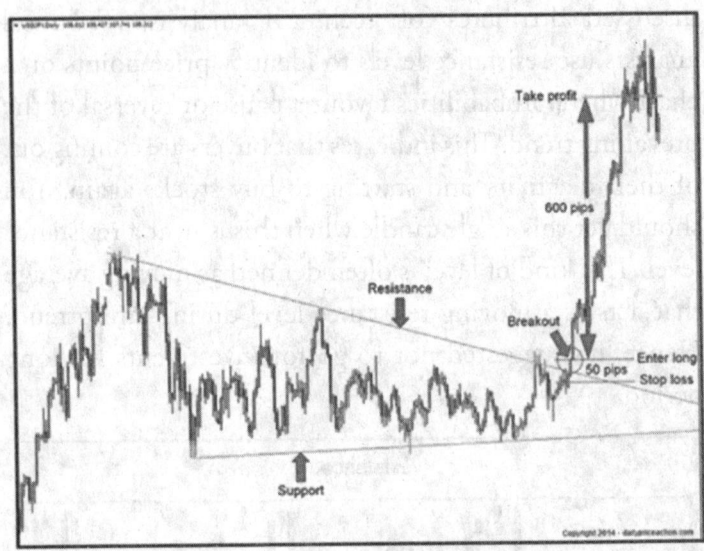

This instrument of technical analysis is the most effective instrument. You have a good chance to make money in support resistance. Many of the investors wait for such signals and they enter the stock once they get such a signal.

Moving Average

- Short Term - 20 days
- Long term - 9 months

Long Term - 9 Months

One, a moving average (MA) is a widely used technical indicator that helps in smoothing out price trends by filtering out the 'noise' from random short-term price fluctuations. It is a trend-following or lagging indicator because it is based on past prices.

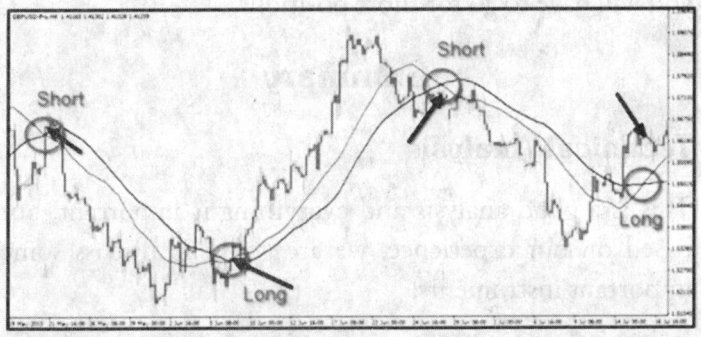

Two, the basic and commonly used moving averages are the Simple Moving Average (SMA) that is simple average of the security for a specific period, and Exponential Moving Average (EMA) that measures further moves up the current prices.

The most common application of moving averages are to identify trend direction and determine support and resistance levels; whereas, moving average are quite useful on their own. As we have wide ranging definitions and articles relating to specific moving averages, we will generally define only the word 'moving average' here.

Simple Moving Average (SMA) is calculated by adding the price of an instrument over a number of time periods and dividing the sum by the number of time periods. The SMA is basically the average price of the given time period, with equal weightage given to the price of each period. When this crosses the bearish trend, you have to go for long positions. If this crosses bullish trend, that means that you will have to go for short positions.

Summary

Technical Analysis

This is a good analysis and everything is important, but based on our experience, we are going to discuss some important instruments.

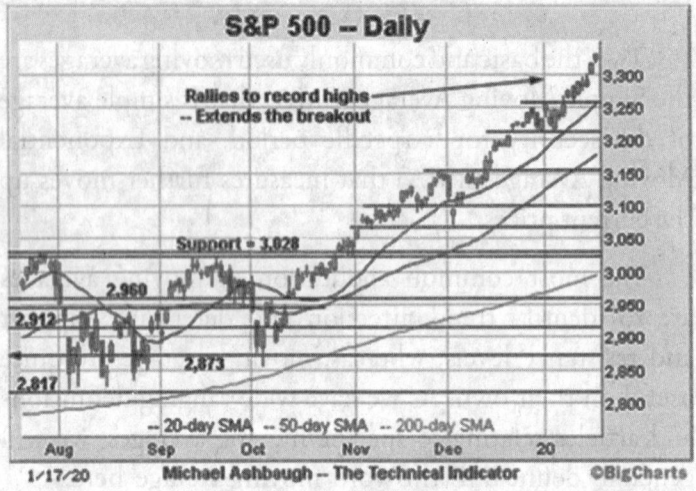

Trend is the best friend. Always invest in the bull trend.

Trend Reversal

A trend reversal is also a good opportunity for investors.

Technical Analysis

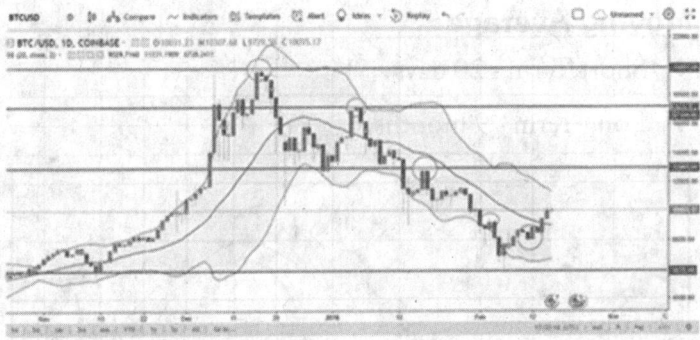

Resistance Breakout

A resistance breakout is a good opportunity also for investment.

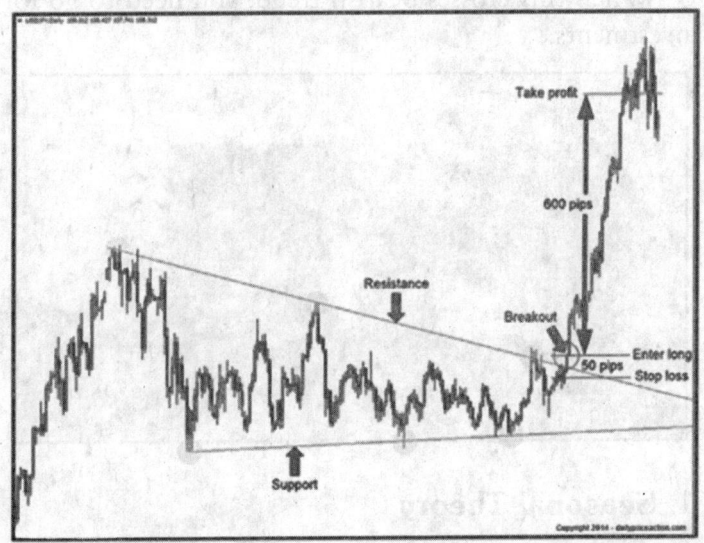

Moving Average
- ❖ Short Term - 20 days
- ❖ Long Term - 9 months

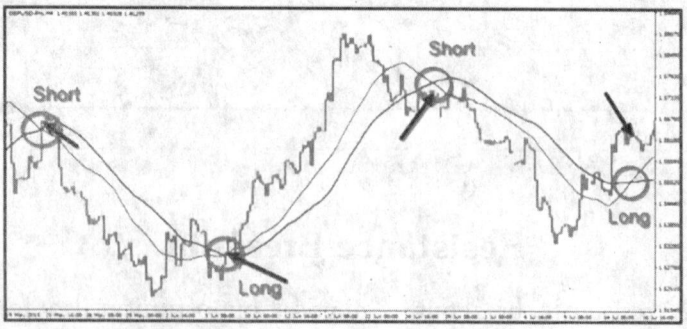

When this crosses bearish trend, you need to go for investments.

1. Seasonal Theory

India has several seasons like - summer, winter, monsoon etc. There are many products that depend on seasons.

Technical Analysis

You would go to buy cotton clothes, T-shirts, cotton bed-sheets, sunglasses, ice creams, air conditioners etc. for summer. You are buying them according to the season - only summer related products in hot weather.

India has winter season also. People would buy products related to winter during cold season. There are many products that are popular during winter like jacket, woollen clothes, heater, thermal inner wear, geyser, suit etc. People are buying products as per seasons. Winter products are selling heavily during winter only. Nobody would buy winter products in summer.

We are working on seasonal theory in the stock market. Under seasonal theory, we would buy stocks of those companies as per the season. Suppose, ice cream is popular in summer; hence we would buy shares of Vadilal Icecreams. Ice cream products are sold from April to June.

We will explain these things properly. We would have to buy the stocks in the month of April and sell the same at the end of June or in the month of July.

Winter will start by October to December. Then, we would buy stocks in October and sell them towards end of December. We would work according to seasons.

❐❐

16

Theory 1: Seasonal Products

Stage 1: Seasonal markets

Stage 2: Identify products

Stage 3: Identify brands and listed companies

Stage 4: Examine fundamentals

Stage 5: Perform technical analysis

Theory 1: Seasonal Products

There are six seasons in a year as per Hindu calendar. Right from the Vedic ages, Hindus of India and South Asia have used this calendar to adjust their lives during the seasons of the year. Religious people, even today, use this for Hindu festivals and other religious occasions.

Theory 1: Seasonal Products

Every season is two months long and important festivals and events are celebrated during all those months. As per Hindu scriptures, there are six seasons -

- ❖ Vasant Ritu: Spring
- ❖ Grishma Ritu: Summer
- ❖ Varsha Ritu: Monsoon
- ❖ Sharad Ritu: Autumn
- ❖ Hemant Ritu: Pre-winter
- ❖ Shishir or Shita Ritu: Winter

The climate of the North India mostly follows these indicated changes in season. These changes are comparatively less exhibited in South India that is located close to equator.

India Has Seasonal Business

What is a Seasonal Industry?

A seasonal industry refers to a group of companies related by their common business activities. They earn the majority of their income during a fairly small number of weeks or months each calendar year. The annual business cycle for these firms is fairly predictable; they have only one or two high points during which customer activity is quite significant.

The rest of the year tends to be either lackluster or unprofitable. For instance, Halloween Company makes ample profit with its business selling costumes and accessories or Christmas trees and ornaments. A seasonal industry is different from a cyclical industry. The experiences of the past predict changes in business patterns each year, while the latter ones see such changes spread out over multiple years.

Understanding Seasonal Industries

Seasonal industries typically ebb and flow along with the annual sales cycle. They must make enough money during their seasonal peaks to last the business owners the entire year; otherwise, these business owners need other sources of income to sustain them during the off-season. While some businesses only stay open for the busy season, such as an ice cream stand, others significantly bring down business activity for the remainder of the year.

Owners of seasonal businesses have to spend considerable time managing their cash flows. Either enough free cash is saved over time as a safety net or a line of credit is secured to cover liquidity issues that may occur outside the busy season.

Workers in seasonal industries often work more than 40 hours a week during the high season.

Stage 2: Identify the Products

Seasonal Products for Summer
Weight Loss and Diet Products

They appear in summer. Bodywash gels etc. come in summer.

Demand for health-related products, especially weight loss products, is good around January (thanks to new year resolutions) and summer.

This, no doubt, is a vast category, but this includes some all-season products. Some of them are -

Juice

There is great demand for fresh or packed fruit juices during summer months. These products have fresh properties and are very good for health.

Protein Powder

Like protein bars, this is one of the most popular sources for protein for fitness-enthusiasts. Its demand goes up around January and summer.

Sunglasses

Obviously, there is great demand for this around summer. People have to go out in sun and hence, they want to keep their eyes protected (and look clam). With healthy life-style being more prevalent now than before, health gadgets have a strong presence among the products that are in demand.

Car Air Purifier

They come in different kinds, shapes and designs. They are generally plugged into car cigarette lighters. Such purifiers are able to minimise dust and other allergy inside your car besides also reducing smells like tobacco or fast food.

Travel Bag

This is an all-season product; world travel is getting popular more and more and hence, demand for travel bags is going up for a long time.

Cotton Clothes

It's comfortable to wear cotton clothes in summer. This also makes it easier to attract like-minded people. Besides this, summer is also a good time to sell cotton clothes for men, women and children. We also use cotton bed sheets, cotton towels and many other cotton clothes during summer.

Ice Cream Making

Ice cream is a product that sells only in summer.

Theory 1: Seasonal Products

Production of Packaged Drinking water

Packed drinking water is also a product having great sales during summer; but is required throughout the whole year.

Air conditioners and Air coolers

Air conditioners and Air coolers are fast selling products in summer.

Business of Cane Juice

Cane juice business is also a high selling business in summer. Body lotions and sun creams are widely used in India.

Tour & Travel Business in Summer

Most of the families plan for travels during summer, as children have their vacations in summer. Many other products are also used in India.

Stage 3: Identify the Brands

Identify the most popular brands manufacturing summer products in India.

Popular brands of ice cream are:

- ❖ Amul
- ❖ Kwality Walls
- ❖ Baskin Robbins

- ❖ Vadilal
- ❖ Havmor
- ❖ Dinshaw's
- ❖ Mother Dairy, etc.

Popular air conditioner brands:
- ❖ Haier
- ❖ Blue Star
- ❖ Voltas
- ❖ Lloyd
- ❖ LG
- ❖ Carrier
- ❖ Hitachi

Popular tour and travel companies in India:
1. Cox and Kings
2. Thomas Cook
3. SOTC
4. Kesari Tours
5. Club Mahindra
6. Expedia
7. Yatra
8. MakeMyTrip
9. Travelguru

Theory 1: Seasonal Products

Cotton (clothes) producing companies in India:

- ❖ Arvind Limited
- ❖ Bombay Dyeing & Manufacturing Company Ltd.
- ❖ Bombay Rayon Fashions Ltd., Fab India Overseas Pvt Ltd, Grasim Industries Ltd. (Aditya Birla)
- ❖ JCT Ltd.
- ❖ Karnataka Silk Industries Corporation Ltd.
- ❖ Raymond Ltd.
- ❖ Lakshmi Mills Company Ltd.
- ❖ Vardhman Textiles Ltd.
- ❖ Products for winter season:
- ❖ Winter clothes
- ❖ Wind Craft
- ❖ Fort Collins
- ❖ Woodland
- ❖ Tommy Hilfiger
- ❖ Puma
- ❖ Decathlon
- ❖ Calvin Klein
- ❖ Monte Carlo
- ❖ Raymond

Thermal brands:
- Jockey
- Lux
- Ice Bear
- Alfa
- Oswal
- Hanes
- Rupa

Stage 4: Check Fundamentals

We will have to check all the lists

We first of all verify whether the brand is a listed company. If the brand is not listed, we can't make investment in that company i.e., we can't buy its shares. Out of the popular brands of ice cream:

- **Amul:** Anand Milk Union Ltd. is not listed.
- **Baskin Robbins:** Baskin Robbins Inc is not listed.
- **Havmor:** Havmor Icecream Company Ltd. is not listed.
- **Dinshaw's:** Dinshaw's Dairy Foods is not listed.
- **Mother Dairy:** National Dairy Development Board has not been constituted.
- **Kwality Walls:** Hindustan Uniliver Ltd. is listed.
- **Vadilal:** Vadilal Industries Ltd. is listed.

Theory 1: Seasonal Products

You may see that only two brands are listed.

- ❖ **Kwality Walls:** Hindustan Uniliver Ltd. is listed.
- ❖ **Vadilal:** Vadilal Industries Ltd. is listed.

Once you filter out the listed products, you will have to examine the fundamentals before making investment. After checking those fundamentals, you may decide if you should go ahead with your investment or not. If the fundamentals are good, you will have to decide to make investment.

Among the popular air conditioner brands:

- ❖ **Haier:** Haier Group Corporation is not listed.
- ❖ **Blue Star:** Blue Star is listed.
- ❖ **Voltas:** Voltas Ltd. is listed.
- ❖ **Lloyd:** Lloyd Electric & Engineering Ltd. is listed.
- ❖ **LG:** LG Electronics Inc is not listed.
- ❖ **Carrier:** Carrier Aircon Ltd. is listed.
- ❖ **Hitachi:** Johnson Controls-Hitachi India Ltd. is listed.

You may see that only two brands are listed.

- ❖ **Carrier:** Carrier Aircon Ltd. is listed.
- ❖ **Hitachi:** Johnson Controls-Hitachi India Ltd. is listed.

Once you filter out the listed products, you will have to examine the fundamentals before making investment. After checking those fundamentals, you may decide if you should go ahead with your investment or not. If the fundamentals are good, you will have to decide to make investment.

Popular tours and travel companies in India:

- **Cox and Kings:** Cox and Kings Ltd. is listed.
- **Thomas Cook:** Thomas Cook Ltd. is listed.
- **SOTC:** SOTC Travel Ltd. is not listed.
- **Club Mahindra:** Mahindra Holiday Ltd. is listed.
- **Expedia:** Expedia Group is not listed.
- **Yatra:** Yatra.com is not listed.
- **MakeMyTrip:** MakeMyTrip is not listed.
- **Travelguru:** Travelguru.com is not listed.

You may see that only three brands are listed:

- **Cox and Kings:** Cox and Kings Ltd. is listed.
- **Thomas Cook:** Thomas Cook Ltd. is listed.
- **Club Mahindra:** Mahindra Holiday Ltd. is listed.

Once you filter out the listed products, you will have to examine the fundamentals before making investment. After checking those fundamentals, you may decide if you should go ahead with your investment or not. If the

Theory 1: Seasonal Products

fundamentals are good, you will have to decide to make investment.

Textile Manufacturing Companies in India

Textile Manufacturing Companies in India

1. **Arvind Limited (Lalbhai):** Arvind Ltd. (Lalbhai) is listed.
2. **Bombay Dyeing Ltd.:** Bombay Dyeing Ltd. is listed.
3. **Fab India Overseas Pvt Ltd:** Fab India Overseas Pvt Ltd. is not listed.
4. **Grasim Industries Ltd.:** Grasim Industries Ltd. is listed.
5. **JCT Ltd.:** JCT Ltd. is listed.
6. **Karnataka Silk Ltd.:** Karnataka Silk Ltd. is not listed.

You can see that only four brands are listed:

- **Arvind Limited (Lalbhai):** Arvind Ltd. (Lalbhai) is listed.
- **Bombay Dyeing Ltd.:** Bombay Dyeing Ltd. is listed.
- **Grasim Industries Ltd.:** Grasim Industries Ltd. is listed.
- **JCT Ltd.:** JCT Ltd. is listed.

Once you filter out the listed products, you will have to examine the fundamentals before making investment. After checking those fundamentals, you may decide if you should go ahead with your investment or not. If the fundamentals are good, you will have to decide to make investment.

Winter Products

Winter Products

- **Wild Craft:** Wild Craft India Pvt Ltd. is not listed.
- **Fort Collins:** Indra Hosiery Mills is not listed.
- **Woodland:** Woodland India is not listed.
- **Tommy Hilfiger:** Tommy Hilfiger is not listed.
- **Puma:** Puma Company is not listed.
- **Decathlon:** Decathlon Sports India is not listed.
- **Calvin Klein:** Calvin Klein is not listed.
- **Monte Carlo:** Oswal Woollen Mills is not listed.
- **Raymond:** Raymond Ltd. is listed.

You can see that only one brand is listed:

- **Raymond:** Raymond Ltd. is listed.

Once you filter out the listed products, you will have to examine the fundamentals before making an investment. After checking those fundamentals, you may decide if you should go ahead with your investment or not. If the fundamentals are good, you will be able to decide about making the investment.

Thermal Brands

- ❖ **Jockey:** Page Industries Ltd. is not listed.
- ❖ **Lux:** Vishwanath Hosiery Mills Ltd is not listed.
- ❖ **Alfa:** Alfa Laval P Ltd. is not listed.
- ❖ **Oswal:** Oswal Woollen Mills Ltd. is not listed.
- ❖ **Hanes:** Hanes Inc is not listed.
- ❖ **Rupa:** Rupa & Company Ltd. is listed.

You can see that only one brand is listed:

- ❖ **Rupa:** Rupa & Company Ltd. is listed.

Once you filter out the listed products, you will have to examine the fundamentals before making investment. After checking those fundamentals, you may decide if you should go ahead with your investment or not. If the fundamentals are good, you will have to decide to make investment.

Stage 5: Perform Technical Analysis

If you have decided to invest after checking fundamentals, you will have to perform technical analysis. We have already discussed about technical analysis.

Check chart patterns and analyse them. If the charts are not showing results as per your requirements, you will have to wait for the right time. Just remember the most important instruments for technical analysis. We are discussing four important points again.

1. **Bull Trend:** Always invest in the bull trend.
2. **Trend Reversal:** Trend reversal from bear to bull is good. A trend reversal is also a good opportunity for investors.
3. **Resistance Breakout:** Resistance Breakout also is a good opportunity for investments.
4. **Moving Average:** Sort Term - 20 days and Long Term - 9 months, when this crosses a bear trend, you will have to go for your investments.

Seasonal Stocks

Summer Products

Vadilal

- May 2018, ₹829
- March 2019, ₹445
- April 2019, ₹580
- 30% appreciation

  2 months - ₹1 lakh appreciated to ₹1,30,337.

Thomas Cook for training

- February 2019, ₹203
- April 2019, ₹256
- 26% appreciation

  3 months - ₹1 lakh appreciated to ₹1,26,108.

Theory 1: Seasonal Products

Bombay Dyeing Cotton

- May 2018, ₹313
- February 2019, ₹99
- April 2019, ₹143
- 44% appreciation
  3 month's projection
- ₹1 lakh appreciates to ₹1,44,450.

Winter Products

- Raymond for suits
- October 2018, ₹600
- December 2018, ₹850
- 40% appreciation
  3 months - ₹1 lakh to ₹1,41,666.

Rupa for thermal wear

- October 2018, ₹242
- December 2018, ₹344
- 42% appreciation
  3 months - ₹1 lakh appreciates to ₹1,42,148.

❏❏

17

Theory 2: Bill Gates

❖ Bill Gates theory suggests focusing on essential products. Bill Gates is the second richest person in the world. Jeff Bezos (owner of Amazon.com) is today the richest person in the world.  Bill Gates continued to be at the first position for so many years. What principles has he adopted? We may follow the characteristics of the richest persons of the world.

When people were focusing on computers, he was paying attention to software. He knows that none of the computers would run without software. The computer is a hardware and a software is needed to make it function. He was focusing on software and building Windows. As you know, Windows is the basic operating system for any desktop or laptop.

Computer companies manufacture computers and buy operating system from his company. There are plenty of companies in the world to manufacture computers and buy software from his company.

Demand for computers that are transforming in shape, is growing day-by-day. Heavy demand for computers keeps the revenue of his company growing and one day, he becomes the richest person of the world.

How can we apply this formula in the stock market?

If we accept that an automobile is an important part of our life, people would buy more automobiles in future for their use and hence, the demand for automobiles would grow in future. What is the essential part of all automobiles?

Automobile companies would manufacture these automobiles. For the automobile companies, tyres and auto parts are the basic products. Then, we have to focus on companies manufacturing tyres and auto parts. Tyres and auto parts are essential parts of an automobile.

All the vehicles need goods. We do not focus on automobile companies; but we may focus on tyre and automobile companies. If we focus on such companies, we would have to check which are the listed companies in that sector. Identify the companies and then check fundamentals. If any specific company has strong fundamentals, go for its technical analysis. Make investment only after applying all formulas.

Let's assume that the population of our country is increasing day-by-day. Food, clothes and housing are the basic necessities. Property is the necessity that people need every day. Land is not growing while population is continuously growing. Hence, the cost of land is moving up and up.

A house is an essential part of our life. People would buy more houses in future for their use and demand for houses would go up in future. Then, business for manufacturing companies would go up. What are the basic elements for manufacturing companies?

Manufacturing companies are the most important part of automobiles. All the vehicles need tyres. If we do not focus on automobile companies, we may focus on tyres. If we focus on tyres, we would have to check which are the listed companies in that sector. Identify the companies and then check fundamentals. If any specific company has strong fundamentals, go for its technical analysis. Make investment only after applying all formulas.

Theory 2: Bill Gates

Shree Cement

- January 2001, ₹57
- January 2009, ₹544
- January 2019, ₹19845
- Had you invested ₹1 lakh in January 2009 - 183 shares @ ₹544, 1 lakh would have grown to ₹36,47,977.
- Had you invested ₹1 lakh in January 2001 - 1754 shares @ ₹19,845, 1 lakh would have become ₹3,48,08,130.

Havells Cable

If you have invested ₹1 lakh:

- April 2009, ₹8
- 12,500 shares @ 8 = 1 lakh
- April 2018, ₹764
- 12500 x 764 - ₹1 lakh grows to ₹95,50,000 in 9 years.

If you have invested ₹1 lakh:

- January 2004, ₹3
- 33,330 shares @ 3 = 1 lakh
- April 2018, ₹764
- 33,330 x 764 - 254 times
- ₹1 lakh grows to ₹2,54,64,120 in 9 years.

Apollo Tyre

- April 2009, ₹15 (6,666 shares)
- April 2018, ₹1251
- ₹1 lakh grows to ₹83,39,999 in 9 years.
- April 2002, ₹7 (14,285 shares)
- April 2018, ₹1251
- 178 times in 16 years - ₹1 lakh grows to ₹1,78,70,535.

Good Year Tyre

- June 2009, ₹93 (1,075 shares)
- April 2018, ₹1251
- ₹1,00,000 grows to ₹13,44,825 in 9 years.

MRF Tyre

- MRF Tyres bought
- ₹1 lakh invested in 2001
- 200 shares @ ₹500
- In 2001, it became
- 200 @ ₹65,000

  It means, in 17 years

- Investment grows 130 times - ₹1,30,00,000

  MRF Tyres bought

Theory 2: Bill Gates

- Invested in 1990
- 6,250 shares @ ₹16 grows to
- 6,250 shares @ ₹65,000
- ₹130 crore in 2018, that means, in 28 years -
- ₹40,62,50,000 - 406 times of invested amount.

MRF Tyres bought

- Investment of ₹3,20,000 made in 1990
- 20,000 shares @ ₹16 grows to
- In year 2018
- 20,000 shares @ ₹65,000 = ₹130 crores
- That means, in 28 years
- ₹3,20,000 invested - 4,060 times.

HDFC Bank

- May 2014, ₹723
- April 2018, ₹2,315
- 300% growth in 4 years
  ₹1 lakh grows to ₹3,20,193.
- May 2008, ₹285
- April 2018, ₹2,315
- 800% growth in 10 years
  ₹1 lakh grows to ₹8,12,280.

April 1990, ₹2

- ❖ April 2018, ₹2,315
- ❖ Grows to ₹10 crore in 28 years
  And, profit from dividends ₹9 lakh approximately.
- ❖ 1000 times return.

❑❑

18

Theory 3: Premium Brands

In this theory, we are trying to explain to you how you can make money by following this theory. Premium brands play a significant role in our economy. When we go to  market and buy a product, we have to ask the shopkeeper which is the premium brand. You further check whether that which majority of people are buying is not a premium brand. If you analyse and find that people are mad about the same, that one is then a good premium brand.

One more point, you might have checked which one is the common brand in that sector and which one is the premium brand in the same. If you are going to buy undergarments, you will have to check which are the brands in the same. You may find brands like Lux, Amul, Rupa etc. and then you find the premium brand Jockey. In comparison to local brands, you generally have to spend some extra amounts for such premium brands.

Here is one more example. You want to buy a motorcycle; you go to a showroom and enquire about the brands available like Bajaj, Honda and Hero. In this sector, Bullet is the product of Eicher Bullet Motors and is also a choice of the generation. This comes with a higher price in comparison to other bikes; hence, this is certainly a premium brand. You can observe what a premium brand means in our life.

Theory 3: Premium Brand Theory

Stage 1: Find out the products

Stage 2: Identify premium brands

Stage 3: Identify brands and listed companies

Stage 4: Check fundamentals

Stage 5: Perform technical analysis.

Eicher Motors Ltd.

₹1 lakh invested in May 2009
- 458 shares @ ₹218
- May 2018 - 458 shares @ ₹32,236

Theory 3: Premium Brands

- 147 times growth in 9 years
  ₹1 lakh grows to ₹1,47,64,088.

  ₹1 lakh invested in April 2001
- 4,545 shares @ ₹22
- May 2018 - 4,545 shares @ ₹32,236
- 1,465 times growth in 17 years
  ₹1 lakh grows to ₹14,65,12,620.

Page Industries Ltd.

₹1 lakh invested in 2009
- 175 shares @ ₹570
- Seo 2018
- 175 shares @ ₹1,35,920
- 63 times in 9 years
  ₹1,00,000 grows to ₹62,86,000.

19

Theory 4: Mass Consumption

Large scale consumption also is one of the most important expectations in the stock market. This mass consumption tells us about  the services and products utilised by common people on large scale. When we go to a mall for shopping, we always try to find out the products that are being used by other people the most.

After this, we will have to recollect all those brands that people are using. We then search for all those brands and companies that most of the people enjoy. We now have to go and work out the details. We then have to find

Theory 4: Mass Consumption

out the company that is linked to that brand. You are then able to realise that brand has started to work on this.

Suppose we are out in the market to buy hair oil. There are many brands for the same; however, we have brought coconut hair oil with brand name Parachute that is commonly used at home. You may also observe that we use few drops of the oil everyday before we comb our hair. The bottle gets empty after several days and we go to market to buy the same again. Then, after some research, you come to know that this hair oil has been manufactured by MARICO Company. Once we identify the company of products, we will have to perform the fundamental analysis for that specific company. After fundamental analysis, we will have to perform technical analysis to find out the entry and exit points.

Let's understand this with another example. Let's assume every household in India has a school-going child who is using notebooks. After some research we come to know that most of the notebooks used by those children are of 'Classmate' brand.

Once we know the brand, we find out that the same is manufactured by ITC Company. We will have to then perform fundamental analysis for the same.

If we find that the fundamentals of the company are strong, we need to perform technical analysis as the final stage of investigation to confirm the entry and exit points.

Following the above theory, you may operate in the stock market quite comfortably in a way that is most appropriate to earn profits. And then, lots of opportunities would be available to you to make money in the stock market.

Theory 4: Mass Consumption

Stage 1: Find out products consumed at large scale

Stage 2: Identify mass consumption products

Stage 3: Identify popular brands and listed companies

Stage 4: Check fundamentals

Stage 5: Perform technical analysis.

4. Theory Mass Consumption

₹1 lakh invested in MARICO in April 2009.

- ❖ 3,448 shares @ ₹29
- ❖ In year 2018 - 3,448 shares @ ₹1361

  ₹1,00,000 grows to ₹12,44,728 in 9 years.

  ₹1 lakh invested in April 2000.

- ❖ 33,333 shares @ ₹3
- ❖ In year 2018 - 33,333 shares @ ₹361
- ❖ 120 times growth in 18 years.

Theory 4: Mass Consumption

₹1,00,000 grows to ₹1,20,33,213.

Dividends of ₹8 lakhs to 9 lakhs received additionally.

ITC

₹1 lakh invested in April 2009.

- ❖ 3,571 shares @ ₹28
- ❖ In year 2018 - 3,571 shares @ ₹305
- ❖ ₹1,00,000 grows to ₹10,89,155 in 9 years.

₹1 lakh invested in April 2000.

- ❖ 33,333 shares @ ₹3
- ❖ In year 2018 - 33,333 shares @ ₹305.
- ❖ ₹1,00,000 grows to ₹1,01,66,565 in 18 years.

❑❑

20

Theory 5: Multi-bagger

What are the parameters to check in a multi-bagger?

- ❖ It's difficult to identify a multi-bagger stock. Investors have to be aware that stocks may be multi-bagger on account of economic factors, development trends of industries, changes in regulatory companies and their fundamentals.

- ❖ Besides the fundamentals of the company, all other factors are mostly unpredictable. Hence, focus should be on fundamentals.

- ❖ Companies that are facing problems trade on lower value and have the possibility of experiencing a change.

❖ Those businesses that operate in sectors that are going through a very strong development phase. Multi-bagger stocks would be mostly from mid-cap and small-cap space and after remaining in 'risk on' mode in the market, have the potential for better performance.

In respect of fundamentals, investors should look out for the companies that are financially strong and operate with positive cash flow, good quality management and lower valuation.

CAN SLIM Theory

The CAN SLIM model - invented by William O'Neil in the United States of America, inspired us. We have put all the listed companies in India on technology-driven automatic screeners and we run these screeners every day. Here are the details:

C: **Current EPS:** It should grow year over year and quarter over quarter.

A: **Actual earnings:** Actual earnings during last three years. This should be within the range of 18% to 25%. Below that, we may ignore.

N: **Novelty or Newness:** This is very relevant and we think has the maximum impact on finding a winner. New products. New management. Even an IPO since new listings provides a lot of room for growth in price. A lot of these stories are under large funds and they are appreciated. They come much later.

S: Shares outstanding: They should be limited in supply and tight. They should not be large issuers of capital. Not serial dilute.

L: Leadership: Which are the stocks out of these 5,000 are relative to one another making lifetime highs. This is an extremely relevant point. It sounds very appropriate; but this part tells us that you need to focus on the leadership. You need to look for value at a 52-week high. Most of the people tend to look the other way, right? We screen for this.

I: Institutional sponsorship: I think in the Indian context it just means that there are some smart money investors already there.

M: Market direction: This is something we don't pay much emphasis to. Is the market in an uptrend or a downtrend? This may actually help you make your purchases a little better.

- ❖ This helps you screen the hot stocks of tomorrow.
- ❖ Definitely, we do a lot of fundamental work after the CAN SLIM screening process is run; but the kind of names that are thrown up are found to have already gone up 4 or 5 times. The typical human mind would say, okay, it was ₹25 three months ago, it's now ₹100. How can you buy this? But some of the biggest gainers – Eicher Motors went from ₹1,000 to ₹10,000; now it's ₹30,000. MRF Tyres went from ₹1000 to ₹10,000 and now

Theory 5: Multi-bagger

it is at ₹70,000. In my view, you will find your biggest winners here. And you know, we've tried to put this in a technology-driven process. It is run daily at the press of a button. We've been working on this for a decade now. So, we keep making improvements to it.

◻◻

21

Tips: How to Become a Billionaire?

100 Crores

If we get a return of 24%,
₹10,00,0000 grows to
₹100 crores in 30 years.

Year	Amount (₹)	Amount (₹)
0	10,00,000	10 lakh
3	20,00,000	20 lakh
6	40,00,000	40 lakh
9	80,00,000	80 lakh
12	1,60,00,000	1.60 crore

Tips: How to Become a Billionaire?

15	3,20,00,000	3.20 crore
18	6,40,00,000	6.40 crore
21	12,80,00,000	12.80 crore
24	25,60,00,000	25.60 crore
27	51,20,00,000	51.20 crore
30	1,02,40,00,000	100 crore

If we get a return of 36%,
₹10,00,0000 grows to
₹100 crores in 20 years.

Year	Amount (₹)	Amount (₹)
0	10,00,000	10 lakh
2	20,00,000	20 lakh
4	40,00,000	40 lakh
6	80,00,000	80 lakh
8	1,60,00,000	1.60 crore
10	3,20,00,000	3.20 crore
12	6,40,00,000	6.40 crore
14	12,80,00,000	12.80 crore
16	25,60,00,000	25.60 crore
18	51,20,00,000	51.20 crore
20	1,02,40,00,000	100 crore

Power of Compounding

- Single investment of ₹10,000
- 25 years - 126 crore with ₹10,000 @ 60%

- 30 years - 191 crore with ₹10,000 @ 50%
- 35 years - 130 crore with ₹10,000 @ 40%
- 40 years - 106 crore with ₹10,000 @ 30%

After following this theory, you would be able to earn good returns in the stock market. Suppose you make an investment of ₹10,000 only and make investments on regular basis, you would get regular return. You would have to apply the principles of compounding and you would receive great returns.

We have shown the tables above. If you get annual return of 30%, you would become billionaire in 40 years. If you get annual return of 50%, it would take 30 years for you to become a billionaire.

You would have to tread your own path to become a billionaire. You will have to take your own decision and you would become a billionaire one day. Always remember the power of compounding. We have to become billionaire at any cost.

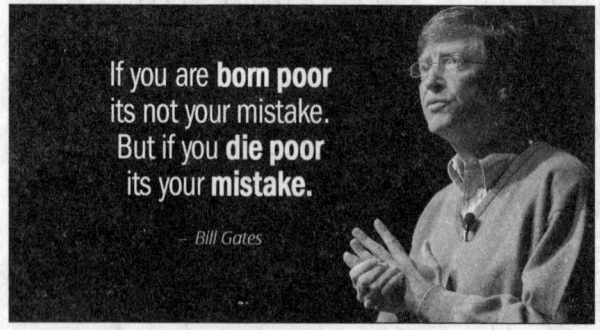